The Clarinet Choir

AF185657

"If only we had clarinets!"

„Ach, wenn wir nur Clarinetti hätten!"

W. A. Mozart (1756-1791)

Friedrich K. Pfatschbacher

The Clarinet Choir

A special form of Ensemble conquers the
world's concert platforms

© 2017 Friedrich K. Pfatschbacher

Cover design and illustration: Friedrich Pfatschbacher
Editor: Friedrich Pfatschbacher
Translation: Nicholas Cox

Publisher: tredition, Hamburg, Germany

ISBN Paperback: 978-3-7439-7412-8

ISBN Hardcover: 978-3-7439-7413-5

ISBN eBook: 978-3-7439-7414-2

Contents

Foreword to the first edition

Since the end of my musical studies in 1990, I have gained considerable experience both as a teacher at the Music School in Mautern and as a clarinettist in a wide range of different chamber music groups. The person who first inspired me to investigate the subject of this work was Prof Dr Wolfgang Suppan. His encouragement coupled with regular musical activity with my own Clarinet Ensemble led me to the decision to write about Clarinet Choirs. Initially, I had intended to tackle the entire repertoire from Duos up to the Clarinet Choir, but very soon I realised the repertoire of Clarinet Duos, Trios, Quartets and Quintets was so enormous, that I decided to limit the scope of the study to the Clarinet Choir itself.

I am particularly indebted to Prof Dr Wolfgang Suppan for his support and encouragement. He assumed the academic supervision in 1999. I would also like to thank my second supervisor Prof Dr Peter Revers for his constructive criticism. I am most grateful to the countless American universities who fielded my enquiries and enabled me to access a large amount of unpublished material. I am also very grateful to my family who have put up with so much!

Friedrich Pfatschbacher   *Carinthia/Austria, December 2017*

Foreword to the second edition

I am very pleased to present a new edition of this book first published in 2005. I have taken the opportunity to include various suggestions and developments in the last ten years. Many new clarinet choirs have been established around the world during this time both in the cultural sector and as training ensembles. This last fact should not however detract from the fact that the clarinet choir as a medium is generally becoming more popular and is emerging as a permanent feature of the concert life in many countries.

In the course of giving concerts at home and abroad with my own ensemble, the *Austrian Clarinet Choir*, I have had the opportunity of getting to know many new arrangements and original works, gaining new inspiration and learning to appreciate the rich possibilities the Clarinet Choir offers.

These days, its tonal palette is not only evident to us connoisseurs. In recent times, the public has started to appreciate the scoring of this unique ensemble ranging from the now well-known E flat clarinet down to the Contrabass Clarinet. While I have seen increased interest in the genre in the course of delivering lectures on the subject in Europe, the USA and South America, it has become apparent that there is hardly any literature on the subject, so it was obviously important to me to have the book translated into English and Spanish and to include as much new information and additional research as I could.

My only hope is that many of you will enjoy this new edition and that it will encourage the establishment of many more clarinet choirs throughout the world.

Introduction

It was only in the last 30 years of the 18th Century that the clarinet attained its permanent position among the family of orchestral instruments. Even after its introduction, clarinet parts were played by oboists in many cases. However the new instrument soon found the wind players necessary to assume its rightful place and bring it to perfection, so that the clarinet's merits and tonal characteristics were quickly recognised. In the realm of military music, the place of the oboe was gradually supplanted by the clarinet. When the Paris Conservatoire was founded in 1795, twelve clarinet teachers were appointed to teach 104 clarinet students. Most of the musicians educated in Paris and elsewhere found posts in military music. Individual wind bands generally consisted of up to 20 clarinettists. According to an English statistic, there were 55,000 clarinettists employed in the regular armies in Europe around this time.[1]

The clarinet's predominance in the period 1770-1830 was achieved as a result of its use as a solo and virtuoso instrument. Then from 1830 onwards, the instrument is mainly encountered in the orchestra and had attained equal status with other instruments. But this 'coming of age' only became apparent after the clarinet's many other merits and tonal possibilities had eclipsed and replaced its rather limited use as a trumpet-like instrument.

Whenever the Clarinet Choir is written about or discussed, the most common observation concerns the limited number of compositions. While this reservation may well be justified, as the extensive repertoire for Clarinet

---

[1] Oskar Kroll, *Die Klarinette* (Reprint of 1965 Edition), Kassel inter alia 1993, pp. 45 – 46; compare with David Whitwell, *Band Music of the French Revolution*, Tutzing 1979 (Alta Musica Vol. 5).

Quartet (3 B flat clarinets and a Bass Clarinet) and Quintet (3 B flat clarinets, Alto and Bass Clarinet) can easily eclipse that of the Clarinet Choir, it was only in the 1920s that the Clarinet Choir itself really emerged in the USA, where its first proper repertoire originated. Even in Europe, it is only since the 1980s that we have been able to observe an increase in the number of new compositions.

In the study of sources, the International Clarinet Association (ICA) Research Center[2] at the University of Maryland, USA deserves a special mention. This library's help was irreplaceable.

Clarinet Choir - News International a trade journal edited by Norman Heim was a true treasure trove of original compositions and arrangements. This trade magazine (of which only seven editions ever appeared)[3] is an important source particularly of contemporary content. Articles that appeared mainly in the magazine *The Instrumentalist* were also very useful.

In the study of sources, the Simeon Bellison Archive at the Rubin Academy for Music and Dance[4] in Jerusalem also deserves a special mention. Bellison was one of the pioneers to address the Clarinet Choir seriously. Furthermore, he directed the Simeon Bellison Clarinet Ensemble from 1927 – 1938, one of the most enterprising and important Clarinet Choirs active in the USA before 1940. Bellison arranged and composed all of the works for his Choir himself.

---

[2] Performing Arts Library, 2511 Clarice Smith Performing Arts Center, University of Maryland, College Park, MD 20742-1630 USA.
[3] acc. information obtained by the author.
[4] cf. Claude Abravanel (Ed.), The Simeon Bellison Archives. At The Jerusalem Of Music And Dance (A catalogue), Jerusalem 1993.

Translator's Note

In translating the German word 'Orchester', I have generally added the word [wind] to clarify instances where the writer is specifically referring to 'wind orchestras'. Where symphony orchestras are implied I have made this clear in the text.

Nicholas Cox

1 The Clarinet Choir

1.1 Development of the Clarinet Choir

The Clarinet Choir's development should be viewed within the broader context of the large clarinet sections in military bands and professional orchestras in Europe, as well as in college and high school bands in the USA. Compositions for Clarinet Choir need to be understood within the narrow context of the clarinet choir's history and its status at that time.

> 'Harmonie music' emerged in the transitional period from the Baroque to the Viennese Classical when the Baroque Orchestra's complete wind section formed itself into its own ensemble, specifically called the 'Harmonie'. The Viennese royal court laid aside the ceremonial pomp of the Spanish royal household adopted by Maria Theresa. Under Joseph II, in place of the Court Orchestra, the 'Royal Chamber Harmonie' appeared, an ensemble of 2 oboes, 2 horns and 2 bassoons, later including 2 clarinets. This group performed a repertoire of original pieces and arrangements and was to become the fashionable ensemble of the day providing entertainment for, as well as representing the aristocracy of central Europe in the last two decades of the 18th Century.[5]

Initially, we encounter this development in the classical Harmonie Music from the second half of the 18th Century. Composed in 1781/82, Mozart's

---

[5] Wolfgang Suppan, 'Woodwind Ensembles in Europe from 15th to 19th Centuries' [Bläser-Ensembles in Europa vom 15. bis in das 19. Jahrhundert], in: *The New Lexicon of Wind Music* [Das Neue Lexikon des Blasmusikwesens], 4th Edition, Freiburg-Tiengen 1994, p. 19; see also ‚Die Harmoniemusik‘, in: *Werk und Wirkung. Musikwissenschaft als Menschen- und Kulturgüterforschung*, ed W. Suppan, Vol. 15, Pt 1, Tutzing 2000, p. 241 ff.

Serenade in B flat KV 370a (KV 360 *Gran Partita*) was written for an ensemble of 13 instruments (not 13 Wind Instruments as is commonly claimed) comprising 2 oboes, 2 clarinets, 2 basset horns, 2 bassoons, 4 horns and Double Bass (Movements: *Largo–Molto Allegro, Menuetto, Menuetto, Romanze, Thema und Variationen, Finale)*. With this work Mozart's output of wind music unquestionably reached its apogee.

In the immediate context of the French Revolution, the Concertante Wind Orchestra grew out of the connection between military field music, Harmonie Music and Turkish music. This was marked by a variable 'choral' scoring of woodwind and brass instruments with the addition of a percussion group.[6]

> The scoring of the *Garde Nationale* Wind Orchestra led by Bernard Sarrette was to become the model of the future military and civil type of wind orchestra. Together with the members of his orchestra, Sarrette founded a music school in 1792. This was renamed the *Institut National de Musique* three years later and then promoted to become the Paris Conservatoire in 1795. At the same time a new type of democratic music school was also established – with pedagogical material produced by teachers which determined the didactics of future teaching based on so-called Vocal and Instrumental Methods (which were also designed for private study).[7]

---

[6] cf. Wolfgang Suppan, *Bläser-Ensembles in Europa vom 15. bis in das 19. Jahrhundert,* loc.cit. p. 20.

[7] ibid, pp. 20–21.

The close relationship established by leading composers and artists with the politicians at this time had made possible the re-organization of the Institute into a more disciplined and permanent institution under the name known today: the Conservatory of Music.[8]

In Germany, the Royal Prussian Guard's Music Director Wilhelm Wieprecht initiated important changes in the area of military music. In the 1830s, Wieprecht and the Austrian Army Kapellmeister Andreas Leonhard helped to develop valved brass instruments in the tenor baritone and bass registers (Tuba and Bombardon). In the first half of the 19th Century, Wieprecht organised the first international meeting of wind orchestras. At a large contest of military music in Paris in 1867, wind orchestras from France (2), Austria, Prussia, Belgium, Spain, Russia, Holland, Baden and Bavaria took part. Wieprecht's wind orchestra then comprised 85 members. Of the 43 wind players, half of them were clarinettists with the following instruments: 1 A flat clarinet, 4 E flat or F clarinets, 16 B flat clarinets (8 1sts and 8 2nds).[9]

It is revealing that Alto and Bass Clarinet are not regular member of the German band.

---

[8] cf. David Whitwell, *Band Music of the French Revolution*, loc.cit. pp. 89–90.

[9] K. E . Nowak, 'A Survey & Analysis of selected Clarinet Choir Literature for Use at the High School Level, A Thesis', Faculty of California State University, Fullerton 1979, p. 22.

Table 1: Military Band of the Royal Prussian Guard Scoring

Instrumental Scoring of the Musikkorps	Prussia	Baden	Bavaria	Austria	Spain	Holland	Belgium	Russia	Garde de Paris	Guides
Piccolo	2	1	1	1	1	1	1	1	1	2
Flute	2	2	2	2	2	-	1	1	2	2
Oboe	3	-	-	-	2	2	2	2	2	3
English Horn	1	-	-	-	-	-	-	1	-	-
Piccolo Clarinet in A flat	1	-	-	2	1	-	-	-	-	-
Piccolo Clarinet in E flat	4	2	4	4	2	2	2	2	4	3
Clarinet in B flat	16	15	10	12	13	10	16	15	8	12
Alto Clarinet (Basset horn)	-	-	-	-	-	-	-	1	-	-
Bass Clarinet	-	-	1	2	-	-	-	1	-	-
Soprano Saxophone	-	-	-	-	-	1	1	1	2	1
Alto Saxophone	-	-	-	-	-	1	1	2	2	2
Tenor Saxophone	-	-	-	-	-	1	1	2	2	1
Baritone Saxophone	-	-	-	-	-	1	1	3	2	1
Bass Saxophone	-	-	-	-	-	-	-	-	-	1
Bassoon	6	2	1	2	3	2	4	2	-	-
Contrabassoon	4	-	-	-	2	-	-	1	-	-
Cornet	4	1	3	2	2	2	2	2	4	4
Trumpet	8	5	8	12	6	4	4	8	3	3
Horn	4	3	5	6	4	4	5	8	2	3
Trombone	8	4	3	6	6	3	4	6	5	5
Little Bugle	-	3	-	-	1	-	-	-	1	1
Bugle	-	3	3	6	2	1	2	-	2	2
Alto Saxhorn	4	1	2	3	2	2	1	-	3	2
Baritone Saxhorn	6	3	1	3	2	2	-	2	2	2
Bass Saxhorn	6	1	-	8	1	2	4	-	5	6
Contrabass Saxhorn (E flat)	-	2	3	-	2	1	2	3	2	3
Contrabass Saxhorn (B flat)	-	3	-	-	2	1	3	3	2	2
String Bass	-	-	-	-	-	3	-	-	-	-
Percussion	6	3	4	5	3	5	2	3	4	1
Total	85	54	51	76	59	51	59	70	60	62

In English wind orchestras at the beginning of the 19th Century, use of the lower clarinets was already commonplace. In his band of 57 musicians, Sir Daniel Godfrey, a graduate of the Royal Military School of Music at Kneller Hall, regularly scored for 20 clarinets. The Clarinet section comprised 4 E flat clarinets, 14 B flat clarinets, 1 E flat Alto Clarinet and 1 Bass Clarinet.[10]

But available sources are less revealing about any standard wind orchestra scoring in the 19th Century:

> Band instrumentation in the nineteenth century was in a state of flux. The size of the bands depended on many variable factors, including official regulations, the depth of the officers' or noblemen's purses, availability of musicians, current fashion, and governmental funding. Bandmaster, especially in the amateur groups, had great freedom and were expected to make arrangements for their own instrumentation.[11]

Even by the early 1920s, it is still not possible to talk about a standard scoring. This is evident from the Ensemble list of the Kneller Hall Band under John Arthur Cowgill Sommerville (1872-1955).[12] Even here there is no scoring for lower clarinets:[13]

---

[10] K. E. Nowak, 'A Survey & Analysis of selected Clarinet Choir Literature for Use at the High School Level, A Thesis', Faculty of California State University, Fullerton 1979, p. 22.

[11] K. E. Nowak, loc.cit. pp. 22–23.

[12] Raoul F. Camus, 'Some Nineteenth-Century Band Journals', in: *Festschrift zum 60. Geburtstag von Wolfgang Suppan*, Tutzing, 1993, p. 336.

[13] Cipolla, F. J., Hunsberger, D., (Hg.), 'The Wind Ensemble and its Repertoire', *Essays on the Fortieth Anniversary of the Eastman Wind Ensemble*, New York 1994, p. 117.

Table 2: Kneller Hall Band Scoring List

Flutes and Piccolos	10	2nd Horns	6
Oboes	6	3rd Horns	5
E-Flat Clarinets	7	4th Horns	4
Solo B-flat Clarinets	13	1st B-Flat Cornets	14
Ripieno Clarinets	7	2nd B-Flat Cornets	10
2nd B-Flat Clarinets	12	1st Trombones	7
3rd B-Flat Clarinets	10	2nd Trombones	6
E-flat Alto Saxophones	4	Bass Trombones	1
B-Flat Tenor Saxophones	4	Euphoniums	12
1st Bassoons	7	Basses	12
2nd Bassoons	5	Tympani	2
1st Horns	6	**Total**	**165**

Gustave Holst's Second Suite was also premiered in this scoring in 1922:

> This was the size of the Kneller Hall Band that gave the premiere per-
> formance of Holst's Second Suite in F for Military Band, Op. 28, No.
> 2, at Albert Hall on 30 June 1922.[14]

And without Alto and Bass Clarinets, the Saxophones assumed more responsibility.

---

[14] ibid. p. 117.

Alto and bass clarinets were eliminated from standard instrumentation as was the B-flat baritone horn. This added a greater amount of responsibility to the saxophones, which were then relative newcomers to the military band.[15]

In the USA in the early 19th Century, the scoring for [military] orchestras [bands] generally only included brass instruments. E flat and B flat Soprano Clarinets were gradually added from about 1830. A recognised scoring with an exact number of clarinet parts wasn't yet standard practice, even though the clarinet parts were increasingly important.[16] One of the first bands which used clarinets independently was the United States Marine Band. The scoring of this band in 1856 comprised 2 E flat Soprano and 4 separate B Flat Soprano clarinet parts.

The expanded use of the soprano clarinets and the introduction and development of the complete clarinet family in the American concert band can be said to begin at approximately the middle of the nineteenth century.[17]

The B flat clarinet was adopted in American Wind Orchestras [bands] from the middle of the 19th Century. Around the same time the Bass Clarinet also appeared in American concert bands for the first time. Going by the sources, this appears to be relatively late, as we know that five Bass Clarinets must already have existed in Hartford, Connecticut in the period from

---

[15] ibid. p. 116.
[16] George D. Stirrat, 'The Development and use of the Clarinet Choir in the American Concert Band', unpubd DMusEd. diss. Columbia University, New York 1968, p. 42.
[17] ibid. p. 43.

1799-1814 and 22 examples had already been built in American work-shops.[18] Again this shows us that brass instruments played a predominant role in American Concert bands well into the middle of the 19th Century.

In Europe, the first reference to a Bass Clarinet is found in the Paris news-paper *L'avant courier* from the edition of 11th May 1772. The reviewer describes the so-called *basse-tube* made by the woodwind maker Gillles Lot in his summary:

> This instrument, in the hands of a skilful artist cannot fail to produce a beautiful effect and should win the approval of the public whether it be heard alone or in the orchestra.[19]

In this context it is worth mentioning Harvey Dodworth, an American in-strument dealer who imported clarinets from Europe and tried to raise awareness of the Bass Clarinet among American concert bands:

> The bass clarinet was the first of the lower clarinets to appear in an Amer-ican concert band. Credit for the introduction of the bass clarinet has been assigned to Harvey Dodworth.[20]

Patrick S. Gilmore was the first bandmaster responsible for giving the clar-inet family real recognition as a section.[21]

---

[18] Johan van Kalker, *The History of the Clarinets* [Die Geschichte der Klarinetten], Ober-ems, 1997, p. 121.

[19] Cited acc David L. Kalinka, 'The structural development of the bass clarinet', DMusEd. diss., Columbia University, 1972, University Microfilms, Ann Arbor, Mich., p. 14.

[20] George D. Stirrat, ibid. p. 43.

[21] ibid. p. 43.

He can be seen as the 'father' of the modern American symphonic wind orchestra. Gilmore's band, the 22nd Regimental Band of New York was considered to be the finest in the country and it encouraged bands across the whole of America to introduce wind instruments into their ensembles.[22] Gilmore was also the first band leader to make the Alto Clarinet well-known and encourage the woodwind sound to predominate.

Gilmore was also the first band leader to make the Alto Clarinet well-known and encourage the woodwind sound to predominate.

> [...] Gilmore was the first American bandmaster to use the alto clarinet in his band. No mention of the existence of this instrument in any band can be found prior to Gilmore. By 1878, the clarinet section in Gilmore's Band consisted of one A-flat soprano clarinets, three E-flat soprano clarinets, sixteen B-flat soprano clarinets, plus one alto and one bass clarinet.[23]

But the size of his band varied. In 1890, it had 21 members and the clarinet section numbered 11 musicians (1 A flat clarinet, 2 E flat clarinets, 7 B flat Clarinets and 1 Bass Clarinet). Two years later, his band had already grown to 100 musicians of which 38 were clarinettists (including 1 A flat soprano, 2 E flat soprano, 30 B flat soprano clarinettists, 2 Altos and 2 Bass Clarinets).[24]

---

[22] cf. Raoul F. Camus, ,The Wind Bands in America from 1759-1918' [Die Blaskapellen in Amerika von 1756-1918], in: *Arbeitsberichte-Mitteilungen der Pannonischen Forschungsstelle Oberschützen* No. 6 (July 1995), pp.47–63; see also, ,The Golden Era' [Das Goldene Zeitalter]. Wind Music in America from 1714-1918 [Blasmusik in Amerika von 1714 bis 1918], in: *Clarino Bläsermusik*, No. 12, from 7-8/2001, pp. 4-8.

[23] George D. Stirrat, loc.cit. p. 44.

[24] ibid. p. 44-45.

After the death of Patrick Gilmore in 1892, another bandleader by the name of John Philip Sousa picked up the threads of this tradition. He assumed the baton of the United States Marine Band in 1880 and raised it to a professional level. In 1892, Sousa founded his own band. At the outset this comprised 49 musicians including the following clarinet section:

2 E flat sopranos, 14 B flat sopranos, 1 Alto and 1 Bass Clarinet.

He then increased the number of instruments gradually until 1924 when his largest ensemble included some 75 musicians. The clarinet section was as follows:

1 E flat Soprano, 1 E flat Alto, 20 B flat Clarinets and 2 Bass Clarinets.

Going by the large number of clarinettists in his band, John Philip Sousa clearly viewed the clarinets as the most important instruments in the woodwind section. Sousa's band influenced not only other professional bands and military wind orchestras, but also university school bands. As a direct result, clarinet choirs gradually began to establish themselves in the universities too. The first leading band at university level was the University of Illinois Band conducted by Albert Austin Harding. This band was, among others, the first university school band to make use of the Alto and Bass Clarinet. In 1906, the Alto Clarinet was introduced and a year later the Bass Clarinet. Only in 1930, 23 years later, did the Contrabass Clarinet make its first appearance in the instrumentarium of the University of Illinois [wind] orchestra. This is the first appearance of the Contrabass Clarinet in an American [wind] orchestra.[25]

This date is corroborated by a comment in Sach's *Handbook of Musical Instruments:*

Recently, (1930!) the Clarinet-Contrabass has also been built by W. Heckel of Biebrich, by Kohl in New York and by Evette and Schaeffer in Paris...[26]

Table 3: University of Illinois Band Scoring development

Significant changes in the Development of the clarinet choir in the University of Illinois Band under Albert Austin Harding													
Instrument	1905	1906	1907	1910	1916	1918	1919	1926	1929	1930	1932	1934	1935	1948
F-flat Clarinet	2		1	1	2	1	1	1	2	1	1	1		
B-Flat Clarinet	12	10	11	17	22	15	19	28	31	30	25	26	28	29
Alto Clarinet		1	1	1		1	2	4	4	4	5	3	5	4
Bass Clarinet			1	1	1	2	2	4	5	4	3	4	4	
Contrabass Clarinet										1	2	3	3	3
Per cent of Clarinets to Total Woodwinds	66	61	64	65	66	60	55	56	54	53	62	65	61	54
Per cent of Clarinets to Winds and Brass	31	26	35	38	34	32	30	35	34	35	38	36	39	34

---

[25] ibid pp. 46-48; see also Raoul F. Camus, loc.cit. p. 4-8.
[26] Curt Sachs, *Handbook of Musical Instruments* [Handbuch der Musikinstrumente], Berlin, 1919, 2/1929. Repr. Leipzig 1930, p. 345.

Other school and college bands included the low clarinets in their instrumentation by 1920. The original instrumentation of the Cass Technical High School Band of Detroit, listed, in 1919, one bass clarinet. In 1920, the band of the University of Wisconsin introduced two alto and two bass clarinets to its instrumentation. An equal number of alto and bass clarinets were introduced into the band of North-western University in 1926.[27]

However the idea of using the clarinet family as an independent ensemble and composing and arranging for it has its roots in Europe:

> Towards the end of the previous century [ie 19th Century], Professor Gustave Poncelet, the clarinet teacher at the Brussels Conservatory had formed an orchestra consisting of 2 E flat clarinets, 5 1sts, 4 2nds and 4 3rd B flat clarinets, 4 basset horns together with 8 B flat clarinets doubling them and 6 Bass Clarinets, a Contrabasset horn and a Contrabass Clarinet.[28]

A report from 1896 by the composer, Richard Strauss, tells us that Professor Gustave Poncelet had performed Mozart's G minor Symphony for him in an arrangement for 22 clarinets.[29] Strauss later noted in his adaptation of

---

[27] ibid. p. 49.

[28] cf. Oskar Kroll, loc.cit. p. 60, Note 2.

[29] Strauss doesn't give this name himself; he is named by the translator Ernest Closson in the French edition of Strauss's Revisions to Berlioz's Treatise on Instrumentation and Orchestration; cf. Richard Strauss, *Le traité d'orchestration d' Hector Berlioz.* Commentaires et adjonctions coordonnés et traduits par Ernest Closson, Leipzig 1909.

Berlioz's Instrumental Method that he very much liked the idea of using the clarinet family as a 'stand-alone' ensemble.[30]

L'idée d'une semblable combinaison me fut suggérée pour la première fois dans une séance du Conservatoire de Bruxelles òu un des professeurs, M. G. Poncelet, me fit entendre la Symphonie en sol mineur de Mozart arrangée pur vingt-deux clarinettes, a savoir:

[The idea of a similar arrangement had been suggested to me for the first time in a performance of the Conservatoire of Brussels Conservatoire, where one of the professors, M. G. Poncelet, made me listen to the G minor Symphony of Mozart arranged for namely 22 clarinets][31]

Table 4: Gustave Poncelet Clarinet Choir Scoring

1 clarinette en la b	2 clarinettes en mi b
12 clarinettes en si b	4 cors de basset
2 clarinettes basses	1 clarinette contrebasse

---

[30] Whether Richard Strauss was really so taken with Poncelet's Ensemble, is doubtful, as he first recalls this in 1905, some 9 years after the publication of the first edition of his Revisions to Berlioz's Treatise on Instrumentation and Orchestration.

[31] Richard Strauss, loc.cit. p. 43.

1.2 Early Clarinet Ensembles in the USA

The Clarinet Choir movement in the USA only really got going with the arrival of the lower clarinets in college and high school bands.[32] In this context the following report by John Morgan about Joseph Schreurs (1863-1941), a very gifted student of Gustave Poncelet, is very illuminating:

Warmelin Clarinet Ensemble

At the time that Schreurs was 1st Clarinet in the Thomas Orchestra in Chicago, Clarence Warmelin, the Principal Clarinettist of the Minneapolis Symphony Orchestra came to have lessons with him. During the lessons he also found out about Poncelet's Clarinet Ensemble and started to show interest in this himself. Warmelin formed his first Clarinet Ensemble while he was teaching in Minneapolis. When Warmelin went back to Chicago, he founded an ensemble of students and local professional musicians. This 'Warmelin Ensemble' ran from 1933-38 or maybe a few years longer. Alongside the clarinet family, Warmelin used almost all instruments of the orchestra in his ensemble depending on the scoring.

His more frequent scoring was:

12 1st B flat Clarinets, 20 2nd and 3rd B flat Clarinets (if necessary he also scored for 4th Clarinets in B flat), Alto Clarinets and Bass Clarinets.

---

[32] However it is not possible to determine definitively which Ensemble was the first, as it has to be assumed that many clarinet teachers must also have organised and experimented with groups [of players]. But the available evidence does not suggest a good reason for the existence of clarinet ensembles before the 1920s.

If required, he also scored for E flat Clarinet, Flute, Oboe, Bassoon, Trumpet, Horn, Trombone, Tuba and Percussion instruments. The two hour rehearsals took place on Sunday mornings. As well as his own arrangements specially written for his ensemble, arrangements from the wind music repertoire were also played. It is worth mentioning that Warmelin himself assumed the whole financial responsibility. One could also describe this Clarinet Ensemble as an experimental ensemble, for no public performances took place or were envisaged. Warmelin gave students the opportunity to experiment and exchange experiences with professional musicians from Chicago. Sometimes guest conductors came to work with the Ensemble. This way they used the opportunity to engage musicians for various jobs, for example in radio broadcasts for Chicago radio station. Or they only needed smaller ensembles to play for a lunch or various clubs etc. From this 'Warmelin Ensemble', the "Warmelin Quartet" was formed, later to become very famous not least through its many performances throughout the USA, on the radio and in recordings.[33]

---

[33] John Morgan, 'The History of the Clarinet Choir', in: Woodwind Anthology. A compendium of Woodwind Articles from *The Instrumentalist*, [Ed.loc.cit.], Vol. 2, Northfield, Ill. 1986, pp. 767–769; see also John Black Morgan, 'The Clarinet Choir', unpubd DMA thesis, University of Michigan, 1962, pp. 22–24.

Simeon Bellison Clarinet Ensemble

This most celebrated and successful Clarinet Ensemble was founded in 1927 by Simeon Bellison (Principal Clarinet, New York Philharmonic, 1921-48). The Simeon Bellison Clarinet Ensemble was the most ambitious, most important and, up to and including the present day, the most unique Clarinet Ensemble. As Bellison conducted it in the decade leading up to the 2nd World War, I would like to examine his role more closely.

Simeon Bellison was born in Moscow on 4th September 1881. At 12 years of age, he entered the Regimental Band of the provincial town of Smolensk under the baton of his father. Vasily Safonov, then Director of the Moscow Conservatory, arranged for him to study there with Professor Joseph Friedrich. He completed his studies at the Moscow Conservatoire in 1903 with the highest honours. As well as his clarinet studies, he completed a special course for Orchestration with the composer Ippolitov-Ivanov. After finishing his study, Bellison served as Principal Clarinet in the Moscow Opera House (the Art Theatre) for the next nine years. From 1915 -18 he was a member of the Imperial Opera House in Petrograd. War, hunger and the gradual spread of the Revolution made it necessary for him to leave Russia. Bellison wrote about his further career:

[...] Once more I organized a chamber music ensemble (strings, piano and clarinet) under the name "Zimro" (meaning singer) and we started out into the world giving concerts everywhere and thus making our way from city to city and from country to country. We crossed Siberia, visited China, Japan, Dutch East Indies, the Philippines, Canada, and finally reached America. In the course of our three-year journey we gave over 200 concerts and in the majority of them, I appeared as soloist.[34]

In 1920, he emigrated to New York and within a year had won the position of Principal Clarinet in the New York Philharmonic Orchestra which he held until 1948. Bellison performed as a soloist with the finest orchestras and chamber ensembles. He gave private lessons and taught in various institutions. Of the several chamber ensembles he founded, the Simeon Bellison Clarinet Ensemble rose to fame. This ensemble played at a very professional level and is still regarded today as an absolute novelty for its time.[35]

The following captures the story of the Simeon Bellison Clarinet Ensemble:

First Bellison started rehearsing with a double quartet (4 Clarinets in B flat, 2 basset horns and 2 Bass Clarinets). In the next two years this ensemble grew into an orchestra of 75 members (Pamela Weston reports that some of the players were women).[36] All of the pieces that were played were arranged or composed by Bellison himself. This ensemble gave many concerts in New York Town Hall and Carnegie Hall (the concert programmes can be seen today in the Rubin Academy of Music and Dance in Jerusalem). The ensemble's last performance took place in New York Town Hall on 27th April 1938.

---

[34] Simeon Bellison, unpubd Article – possibly for the New York Philharmonic Orchestra, in: *The Simeon Bellison Archives at the Jerusalem Rubin Academy of Music and Dance*, A Catalogue, ed. Claude Abravanel, Israel 1993, p. 5.
[35] ibid. p. 5.
[36] cf. P. Weston, More Clarinet Virtuosi of the past, Suffolk, England 1992, p. 47.

The Bellison Ensemble played with the following scoring:

Piccolo Clarinet in A flat, E flat and B flat Clarinets and Basset horns, Alto Clarinets and Contrabass clarinets, to which Bellison added brass and percussion instruments as well as harp and harmonium.[37]

In an unpublished article dating from 1935 Bellison gave us more precise details about the origins of his clarinet ensemble:

> In 1926 four pupils of Mr. Bellison's class played a clarinet quartet by Crosse. The musical success of this unusual combination inspired Mr. Bellison to organize an ensemble which could include the entire clarinet family, from the A flat piccolo to the contrabass clarinet. There were, however, many insurmountable difficulties. For example, some of the instruments, such as the A flat piccolo, bassethorn and contrabass clarinet could not be gotten in America. Also there is no printed literature for a purely clarinet group. Thirdly, the expense was so great that it almost caused the abandonment of the idea entirely.

> In 1927, The New York Symphonie Orchestra merged with the Philharmonic. The later organization continued the scholarships given to talented students of the New York schools. The Committee on Ensemble Musical Training and Scholarships of the Philharmonic Symphony Society of New York invited Mr. Bellison to accept a class of six pupils. As an experienced clarinettist, he knew that individual practise would not make a finished orchestra player, that ensemble playing was necessary. There again the idea of a clarinet ensemble forcefully presented itself.

---

[37] cf. P. Weston, loc.cit. p. 47.

[…] Mr. Bellison now presented his idea to the Committee on Ensemble Training. They were interested enough to furnish him with the necessary funds to procure instruments for a beginning.

By the end of 1928, the ensemble of sixteen players had already given two recitals. In the following year the Committee provided Mr. Bellison with additional funds with the result that remainder of the necessary instruments were purchases in France.

To the ensemble was now added a harp, timpani, trumpet and concertina, also from the scholarships students. This added colour made in a very original unit, which now numbered thirty players. Appearances now began at private and public concerts, which attracted the attention of both public and press.

The artistic playing of the ensemble began to draw clarinettists and other instrumentalists to seek to join the ensemble with the result that it now numbers fifty-seven players.[38]

A concert programme from the 1937/38 season shows that his ensemble consisted of 68 members with the following scoring:[39]

---

[38] Simeon Bellison, unpubd Article – possibly for the New York Philharmonic Orchestra, in: *The Simeon Bellison Archives at the Jerusalem Rubin Academy of Music and Dance*, A Catalogue, ed. Claude Abravanel, Israel 1993, pp. 6–7.

[39] ibid. p. 7.

Table 5: Bellison Clarinet Ensemble 1937/38 Scoring

Piccolo clarinet in A flat	1
Sopranino clarinet in E flat	1
1st Clarinets in B flat	10
2nd Clarinets in in B flat	8
3rd Clarinets in B flat	6
Clarini (4th Clarinets) in B flat	11
Bassett horns	4
Alto clarinets	2
Bass clarinets	6
Contrabass clarinets	2

Trumpets	4
Harps	3
Timpani	2
Concertina	1
Percussion	2
Xylophon	1
Guitar	1
Piano	2
Celesta	1
Harpsichord	1

Essentially the Ensemble retained the same scoring until its dissolution in 1938.

Plate 1: Bellison Clarinet Ensemble[40]

The Bellison Clarinet Ensemble, 1936. Kalman Bloch leading, with David Weber on his left, Leon Russianoff behind Weber. *(Kalman Bloch, Los Angeles)*.

The following review of Bellison Ensemble's anniversary concert at New York Town Hall appeared in the New York Times on 21st March 1937:

> The character of sound produced by the ensemble was unique and had a decided charm and appeal, the preponderance of woodwind tone giving it quite an eighteenth century tang. Under Mr. Bellison's able baton, the young musicians played with an exhilarating enthusiasm and a correctness and elasticity that were a constant delight.[41]

---

[40] cf. Pamela Weston, *More clarinet Virtuosi of the past*, London 1977 (Reprinted 1982), Plate 3.

[41] cf. New York Times, 22nd. March 1937, p. 26.

Since the end of the Bellison Ensemble in 1938, we can still state confidently that there has never been such a famous or extraordinary clarinet ensemble before or since. It also played an important role in New York musical life over a considerable period.

John Geanacos

In his article 'the History of the Clarinet Choir' and his Ph.D Thesis The Clarinet Choir, John Morgan mentioned another Clarinet Choir which was active on the West Coast of the USA around the time of Bellison, just before the so-called 'balanced clarinet choir movement' of 1952.[42]

This ensemble was conducted by the then renowned pedagogue John Geanacos. As sources on this are scarce, we only know these details: the clarinet choir's rehearsals took place on Saturday mornings in John Geanacos's house in San Francisco. It is also worth mentioning that Geanacos wrote all of the arrangements himself.[43] This ensemble should probably be listed earlier as it was evidently founded before 1950.

---

[42] This term was coined by Hal Palmer in 1952, see below.
[43] cf. J. Morgan, loc.cit. p. 768; cf. also loc.cit. p. 31.

1.3 The Balanced Clarinet Choir Movement in the USA

In the 1930s and 40s, the wish to acquire a blended clarinet sound within symphonic wind orchestras in the USA laid the foundations for the development of a standard instrumentation. Experiments of leading composers, conductors and arrangers with the role of the clarinet family in the concert band were also decisive in the development of the clarinet choir as a standalone ensemble.

In the development of clarinet ensembles in the 1950s, teachers and arrangers such as James P. De Jesu, Russell Howland and Harold Palmer were the first to adopt the term 'Choir' instead of ensemble. Through their engagement in arranging the music of significant composers and the publication of these works, other ensembles succeeded in discovering playable repertoire.[44]

In the Winter 1950-5 edition of the Journal *The Clarinet*, a photo and caption first appeared of James P. De Jesu, a busy Long Island teacher with his clarinet ensemble. Jesu was one of the first pioneers who experimented with the clarinet choir. This was the first mention of a clarinet ensemble in a national journal since the famous Bellison Ensemble. In 1951, in the journal *Symphonie*, Lucien Cailliet wrote the first article about the clarinet choir in which he maintained that there was greater hidden potential in a clarinet ensemble than in the already familiar and popular saxophone choir. Then in October 1952 in the journal *The Instrumentalist*, the first reference

---

[44] cf. N. Heim, 'The Development of the Clarinet Choir in the USA', in: *Bericht über die zweite internationale Fachtagung zur Erforschung der Blasmusik*, Tutzing, 1977, pp. 109-110 (Alta Musica 4).

is made to the term 'Clarinet Choir' in an article entitled 'Improved Clarinet Section via Choirs'.[45]

In 1952, Harold Palmer devised the term 'balanced clarinet choir'. His interest in clarinet choirs resulted from his contact with Russell Howland at Fresno State College, California. He gave Howland the job of organising a clarinet choir at the High Plains Music Camp in Hays, Kansas. In an interview between Kenneth Edward Novak and Russell Howland about the development and organisation of the High Plains Music Camp and his work at California State University, we learn that Russell Howland began to make various arrangements of well-known composers' works as there was no suitable repertoire for clarinet choir. Gradually he formed his own clarinet choir:

> With the increased production of bass and contra bass clarinet along with the many clarinettists available, Mr. Howland developed a large clarinet choir. This consisted of an average membership of ten first, second, and third Bb soprano clarinets, ten alto clarinets, eight bass clarinets and eight contra bass clarinets.[46]

Howland began to develop his work from the High Plains Music Camp in Hays at the music department at Fresno, where he composed and arranged for the clarinet choir. Today his works still belong among the finest in the clarinet choir repertoire. Many of them have been published by Rebo Music Publishers and Interlochen Press. The works and experiments in 1952 with

[45] cf. James De Jesu, 'Improved Clarinet Section Via Choirs', in: Woodwind Anthology. A compendium of Woodwind Articles from *The Instrumentalist*, Vol. 2, Northfield, Ill. 1986, p. 665.

[46] cf. Kenneth E. Nowak, loc.cit. p. 31.

the Clarinet Choir in Hays represent, as it were, the birth pangs of the first really well-balanced clarinet choir.

In *The Instrumentalist* in 1955, George E. Waln defined the clarinet choir:

> [...] what is meant by the phrase Clarinet Choir or Balanced Clarinet Choir. It means, simply, the use of the entire family of clarinets in such proportions as to furnish the basic sound of the band, just as the string section provides the basic sound of the orchestra.[47]

As high school and college bands gradually began to fill the ranks of their lower registers, interest in stand-alone clarinet choirs increased.

One of the first pioneers to recognise the potential of clarinet choirs early on, was Don McCathren, Director of Research and Pedagogy at the G Leblanc Corporation from 1953-58 (more about him later). At this time, McCathren recruited Alfred Reed to his movement. Together they toured all across the USA and helped with the organisation and pedagogy in the establishment of new clarinet choirs:

> One of the first American composers to become vitally interested in the clarinet choir and to advocate its use as the basic choir in the concert band was Alfred Reed. Like Gillette, Reed has certain fundamental ideas which he considers essential if the instrumentation of the concert band is to become standardized and balanced ...[48]

---

[47] cf. George E. Waln, 'The Clarinet Choir', in: Woodwind Anthology. A compendium of Woodwind Articles from *The Instrumentalist*, [Ed], Vol. 2, Northfield, Ill. 1986, p. 683.
[48] George D. Stirrat, loc.cit. p. 68.

The above mentioned pioneers set the tone for the phenomenal further development of the clarinet choir movement in 1955 and this was clearly deserved. In June that year, McCathren was invited to conduct at the 'Kansas All-State Music Camp' and later that summer he met up with Russell Howland and Harold Palmer at High Plains Camp.[49]

The following year, McCathren extended his lectures and guest conducting in new parts of the country. He organised and directed clarinet choirs for special occasions like music teaching conferences. One such conference took place on 16th February 1956 at Ball State Teachers College where McCathren organised a choir of more than a hundred clarinettists from high school students from around Muncie, Indiana.[50]

For his lectures McCathren adopted the following plan:

1. First he explained the philosophy of the clarinet choir.

2. With the help of the clarinet choir present, he introduced the various members of the clarinet family and initiated a discussion from the podium.

3. Referring to the inclusion of the lower clarinets, he demonstrated the deep and fascinating tone colour of the clarinet choir.

4. Finally they gave a concert of original pieces for clarinet choir and transcriptions.

---

[49] John B. Morgan, loc.cit. p. 37.
[50] Correspondence between Don McCathren and John B. Morgan from 27.09.1961; cf. J. B. Morgan, 'The Clarinet Choir', loc.cit. p. 38.

Some of the many pioneering 'clinics' delivered by McCathren took place in the following US states:

- ❧ Kentucky State Meeting, Louisville (June 1956)
- ❧ Texas Music Educators Meeting, Dallas (February 1956)
- ❧ Nebraska State
- ❧ Mid-West Band Directors Clinic, Chicago
- ❧ Iowa Bandmasters, Sioux City
- ❧ MENC (National Association for Music Education) regional meeting, Buffalo NY (1959)[51]
- ❧ 11th Band Directors' National Conference, Ann Arbor, Michigan (Summer 1960)
- ❧ Maryland State Meeting, Buffalo, NY (with Alfred Reed)
- ❧ Western Reserve University Clinic, Cleveland, OH

---

[51] MENC: The National Association for Music Education.

Plate 2: Don McCathren at the Texas Music State Convention[52]

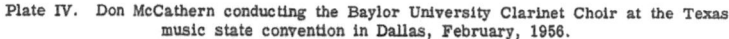
Plate IV. Don McCathern conducting the Baylor University Clarinet Choir at the Texas music state convention in Dallas, February, 1956.

The first original work *Havana Moon* for clarinet choir and percussion, by Alfred Reed appeared in print in 1955 from Leblanc. The composer talked to the current author about the work's origins at the International Mid-

---

[52] J. B. Morgan, loc.cit. p. 40, Plate IV.

European Conference for Symphonic Bands and Wind Ensembles in Schladming, Austria in 2001:[53]

> The three movement *Caribbean Suite* appeared first in manuscript in 1955 from which Charles Hansen published the movement called *Havana Moon*. Actually this work wasn't just for clarinet choir but had three added easy percussion parts. This work is now available from Masters Music and Kalmus.

Havana Moon now belongs to standard clarinet choir repertoire.[54] In the 1950s the composer also made following revealing remark in the score about the development of repertoire for clarinet choir:

> With the development of the Bb Contra-Bass Clarinet, as well as the improvement of the Eb Alto and Bb Bass Clarinets by the G. LeBlanc Instrument Corporation, the Fully Balanced Clarinet Choir, at last, becomes a practical reality. We now have the pure, basic tone for the Band as a complete section in itself, capable of being detached from the Orchestra as a whole, and playing its own literature. The publication of the Caribbean suite for clarinet choir marks the first step in the development

---

[53] Alfred Reed was invited as a Lecturer and Guest Conductor to the 4th Mid-European (The International MID EUROPE Conferences for Symphonic Bands and Wind Ensembles) in 2001 in Schladming, Austria.

[54] This piece was performed in 1995 by the Tokyo Kosei Wind Orchestra conducted by A Reed on the CD Mini winds: Chamber Music for Winds. Available from Kosei Publishing Company; cf. D. M. Jordan, A. Reed. *A Bio-Bibliography*, Westport, Connecticut and London 1999, p. 155.

of a literature for the Band that small stand in the same relationship to it as the String Orchestra literature to the symphonic Orchestra.[55]

Russell Howland made the following statement concerning the financial challenges in organising and founding the College Clarinet Choir at Fresno State College in the 1950s:

> By the fall of 1956, our college budget had come providing for some contra-clarinets and I started a choir here.[56]

As Howland arranged all the works for his choir himself and was considered to be one of the most talented [arrangers] in the land, this benefited other existing choirs as they already had repertoire to play and attractive musical material for the medium.

The Iowa State University Clarinet Choir was founded by Thomas A. Ayres (1955-1958). An enormous force for this new movement across the whole of Iowa, Ayres was a significant driver of the clarinet choir initiative. Another example demonstrates how rare published works [for clarinet choir] were at this time. At a 'Clinic' held at Cedar Rapids, Iowa from 16th-18th January 1958, George Waln from Oberlin College had 26 works at his disposal produced by 9 different publishers.

When McCathren relinquished his post at G. Leblanc Corporation and became Director of Bands at Duquesne University in Pittsburgh, the clarinet choir he set about organising was reputed to be one of the best in the coun-

---

[55] A. Reed, Observations of the Composer, in: Score of Havana Moon, Kalmus & Co., Inc., Boca Raton 1955, p. 8.

[56] Russell S. Howland, 'Forming a Clarinet Choir', in: *Woodwind World*, [Ed], 15th September 1960, pp.

try. Among other performances, this Choir appeared at the Regional Meeting of the MENC in Buffalo on 24th January 1959. In May that year, a photo of the Duquesne Clarinet Choir appeared on the title page of *The School Musician* magazine, creating much excitement among the woodwind circles.[57]

Lucien Cailliet, whom McCathren succeeded as Musical Director for Leblanc in Kenosha, could not have been a bigger catch for the clarinet choir movement. He wrote several articles about the movement at this time, arranged countless works and composed an original piece entitled *Clarinet Poem* (many arrangements and original compositions of Cailliet have subsequently been published).[58]

Russell Howland also provided a considerable stimulus to the clarinet choir movement by organising the first 'businessman's choir'. The members of the ensemble were all adults from the area around Fresno, CA. College students were not allowed to take part in this ensemble, although the School Choir and Business Choir promoted their concerts together. Both choirs each were made up of 40 members in total.[59]

In 1959, there was increased interest in writing for clarinet choir. For example, *A Study in Lavender* a work by Eric Osterling became so popular that an orchestral arrangement had to be made, making it the first [clarinet choir work] to be transcribed.

---

[57] J. B. Morgan, loc.cit., p. 42.
[58] Cailliet is considered to be a champion of the E flat Clarinet scoring for it successfully in his instrumentation. The first Arrangers like R. Howland und J. De Jesu also tried to integrate this instrument [into their scores], but with demonstrably less success.
[59] R. Howland, loc.cit. pp.

In the context of the development of the clarinet choir movement, the Tri-State Music Festival which took place on 1st May 1959 at Enoch, Oklahoma was also very interesting. On this occasion, Don McCathren organised a clarinet choir of 88 members, who had come together from all over the Southern States. This ensemble was featured prominently in the main festival programme. In a subsequent letter to John Morgan, Don McCathren informs us about the event and the rise in popularity of clarinet choirs in schools:

> At the famous Tri-State Music Festival held in Enid, Oklahoma, in May 1959, I organized a high school clarinet choir which made up of 88 clarinet players from throughout the South. This group rehearsed during the festival and played on the festival concert. I believe that the participation of many clarinet players in clarinet choirs at this time built interest in the idea, and these players returned to their high schools enthusiastic and eager for clarinet choir of their own. In addition to this, hundreds of bands and orchestra directors heard these ensembles and were motivated in organizing clarinet choirs in their schools. I sincerely believe that there is no finer way to improve a band than to have an outstanding clarinet choir, since the clarinets are the most important section of the band.[60]

McCathren was also privileged to conduct world premieres of pieces for clarinet choir, notably at the Mid-West National Clinic in December 1960. Here Alfred Reed's work *Clarinet Valsante* received its first performance played by the Searl Pickett Clarinet Choir from Fond du Lac, Wisconsin

---

[60] Correspondence between Don McCathren and J. B. Morgan from 4.11.1961; cf. J. B. Morgan, 'The Clarinet Choir', loc.cit. pp. 44–45.

conducted by the above named conductor. As the organisers of the Mid-West performances of clarinet choirs took them under their wings, on 22nd December 1961, Lucien Cailliet had the opportunity to conduct a programme of his own compositions and arrangements with a 'fully balanced clarinet choir' of students from VanderCook College of Music in Chicago.

Another very successful clarinet choir at the beginning of the 1960s was the ensemble from Lebanon Valley College in Anville, Pennsylvania. Under their then enthusiastic director and teacher Frank E. Stachow, this group appeared at several national teaching conferences. Frank Stachow wrote about the development of his clarinet choir:

> Our Clarinet Choir began originally as a B-flat Clarinet quartet. After a year or so, we resurrected and had overhauled an alto and a bass clarinet. We then operated for a couple of years as a Clarinet Sextet. We then brought a b-flat contrabass clarinet and decided to investigate the possibility of multiplying players on each part. We have since been able to persuade the administration to purchase an additional three alto clarinets, and two bass clarinets, so that our group now varies from 4 to 6 players on each of the first three B-flat clarinet parts; 4 to 6 alto players; 3 to 6 bass players, depending on whether or not we can fill out the sections with interested, competent high school students. So far, this has been possible. This group has performed in the past several years for the various district festivals held in this state, the local Pennsylvania Music Educators Association state convention, and the last year we were privileged to play the Eastern division Convention of the MENC held in

Washington… We also were privileged to play for the national convention in Atlantic City of the NEA.[61]

As previously mentioned, high school and college bands wanted to improve their clarinet sections in the 1950s. This explains why so many engaged and experienced music teachers founded clarinet choirs and therefore had a leading role in the establishment and spread of clarinet choirs. Alongside McCathren and Alfred Reed the following outstanding pedagogues should be mentioned:

- Harold Harvey, Montana State University
- Arthur Christman, Julliard School of Music New York
- William Stubbins, Michigan State University
- Thomas Ayres, Iowa State University
- George Waln, Oberlin State University
- Frank Stachow, Lebanon State University[62]

Committed musicians and Professors with professional choirs from other universities who made contributions to the positive development of the clarinet choir movement in the 1960s include among others:

- Vance Jennings, Wichita State University
- William Willett, New York State University
- David Hite, Capital University
- Harvey Hermann, University of Illinois

---

[61] Correspondence between Frank Stachow and John B. Morgan from 13.12.1961; cf. John B. Morgan, loc.cit. p. 46.
[62] cf. J. Morgan, loc.cit. p. 768.

This second period in the 1960s was marked by an increase in public performances by clarinet choirs. As a consequence of the large music [teaching] conferences, 'clarinet choir clinics' were organised by McCathren, Alfred Reed, George E. Waln and Frank Stachow among others. This explains how a clarinet choir came to play for the first time at the New York World's Fair in May 1965, at the MENC National Convention in New York in May 1966 and even at Expo 1967 in Montreal.

In the course of this decade, several prominent composers like Gordon Jacob, Arthur Frackenpohl, Ivar Lunde, Elliot DelGorgo, Vaclav Nelhybel, William Presser and Howard Rarig wrote works for clarinet choir.

To foster the interest in composing new works for clarinet choir in the 1970s, the publisher Kendor Music Inc promoted a composition competition in collaboration with the University of Maryland for the first time. The winner received $300 and a guarantee that the prizewinning work would be published. The first competition was held in 1975 and attracted composers from the USA, Canada and England. Altogether 37 works were submitted. The jury awarded the honour in this competition to Ivar Lunde Jr from the University of Wisconsin for his work *Nuances*.

The following year a second competition was held. Out of 21 submissions, the prizewinning piece was *Dodecaphonic Study* by Elliot Del Borgo, Professor at Potsdam State College, New York. The composition style of the participating composers ranged from the Romantic to the odd dissonant piece.[63]

---

[63] N. Heim, loc.cit. pp. 109–111.

The following factors contributed hugely towards the further spread of the clarinet choir movement in the USA:

1. Interest in instrumental music increased rapidly in the USA

2. The large scoring, full sound and versatility of the choir

3. The technical improvement of the instruments – particularly the E flat, E flat Alto and B flat Contrabass Clarinets were considerably technically improved

4. With the emergence of the clarinet choir from within its own ranks, the symphonic wind orchestra itself was able to make qualitative improvements

5. Very high quality repertoire was written for clarinet choirs and

6. Considerably better trained and educated clarinettists came to the fore in the USA[64]

To summarise, we have firmly established that the clarinet choir in the USA existed primarily in the education sector. Teachers and conductors recognised the importance of the clarinet choir mainly as an educational ensemble for young students but also as a stand-alone ensemble.[65] Norman Heim, one of the great pioneers of this movement, wrote in 1979 about the clarinet choir:

---

[64] cf. R. K. Weerts, 'The Clarinet Choir As A Functional Ensemble', in: Woodwind Anthology. A compendium of Woodwind Articles from *The Instrumentalist*, [Ed above], Vol. 2, Northfield, Ill 1986, pp. 800–801; cf. N. Heim, loc.cit. pp. 109–111.

[65] Correspondence between F. Pfatschbacher and A. Reed from 25.8.2002.

[…] today, the clarinet choir still serves as a training group for the clarinet section of the symphonic band, since the medium is relatively new. However, the choir is increasingly serving as a performing group with its own literature and concerts. Clarinet choirs are found in the elementary, junior and senior high schools and in many colleges and universities…[66]

The many tonal and scoring options offered by the clarinet choir, allow us to hope that in future, clarinet choirs will make a name for themselves as stand-alone ensembles rather than merely serving the standards of the education sector.

---

[66] N. Heim, loc.cit. pp. 109–111.

1.4   The Clarinet Choir in the 21st Century

Having emphasised that the roots of clarinet choirs were to be found in the school wind music in the USA, in the next chapter I will try to demonstrate the role the clarinet choir plays as a medium for musical expression in the 21st Century.

The function of the individual instruments within the ensemble was also examined in a study dating from 2003-04. In this research project, a questionnaire consisting of a combination of general, specific and open questions was put together and distributed to representative clarinet choirs and their conductors at schools and universities in the USA, Europe, Japan and Australia. The questionnaire was framed so as to allow respondents to answer the questions quickly and precisely. In addition, clarinet choir directors were given the option of making their own statements and sharing their opinions. The study focussed of course mostly on the USA, but only selected clarinet choirs there were approached.

In this context, Raoul F.Camus wrote about wind music in American schools:

> Almost every college has some kind of music on offer. Many important universities have conservatories or 'Schools of Music' which are roughly equivalent to [German] Music High Schools. The University of Indiana for example has over 1200 music students. The larger schools have several different wind orchestras: often a football marching band of up to 300 musicians, a symphonic wind orchestra, various smaller concert

wind orchestras/bands, 'Pep'- Elan wind bands for basketball games and other sporting activities, as well as a specialised wind ensemble.[67]

However, the majority of clarinet choirs were set up for pedagogical reasons as an subsidiary offer to music study at the above mentioned schools and they rarely perform in public. In Europe, the first clarinet choir to be established was the Ionian Clarinet Choir formed in Great Britain in November 1970. It was founded by the musical director Ray Upton Holder in Whetstone in the London Borough of Barnet. Further evidence also suggests this ensemble produced the first recording by a European clarinet choir. Norman Heim also mentioned in his article on the Ionian Clarinet Choir that the BBC and London Broadcasting Company radio stations broadcast various tracks from this recording.[68] On the ensemble's second recording, they performed the Finale from Tchaikovsky's Violin Concerto with Anton Weinberg as soloist.[69]

The first broadcast recording of a clarinet choir in Europe can be dated to 23rd November 1979 (in Zürich):

On November 23, 1979 the recording made by the University of Maryland Clarinet Choir was played on Radio Zürich on its hour featuring wind music. The response of listeners in Switzerland, Austria, and Germany was gratifying. This was the first broadcast of a clarinet choir in Europe.[70]

---

[67] cf. Raoul F. Camus, ‚Wind Music in American Schools' [Blasmusik an amerikanischen Schulen], in: *Clarino*, Vol. 12, No. 11, November 2001, pp. 10–13; citation: p. 12.

[68] It has not been possible to confirm when this recording was broadcast.

[69] cf. N. Heim (Ed.), in: 'Clarinet Choir'. *News International*, No. 2, Spring 1979, p. 6.

[70] N. Heim (Ed) loc.cit. No. 4, Spring 1980, p. 1.

In the rest of Europe, the first clarinet choirs were founded in Belgium and Holland in the 1980s. As the clarinet choir has now established a firm place in the musical landscape of these countries, I will now focus my attention beyond Europe to demonstrate how far the clarinet choir movement has progressed.

Alfred Reed has been regularly invited as a guest conductor to Tokyo for several months of the year and informed the author about the situation with clarinet choirs in Japan and the rest of Asia:

> I would say that this type of performing organization exists largely in the educational area: schools, colleges and universities, much the same as in the U.S. But there are one or two professional organizations which play a few public concerts each year ...[71]

Writing about the functionality and development of clarinet choirs in the USA and Japan, Reed commented:

> Smaller clarinet groups are an important part of the music education system both in Japan and the U.S.: i.e. trios, quartets, quintets, etc., and he larger clarinet choir such as the ones mentioned above has been developing during the past 35 years in both countries, both in the schools and as an amateur group for private performance and enjoyment.[72]

---

[71] cf. Alfred Reed, loc.cit.
[72] ibid.

While one might expect that a clarinet choir movement is now underway in South Africa,[73] my research has only been able to uncover patchy evidence. However a report from Spencer Pitfield about the College of Music in Zimbabwe shows that the provision of a clarinet choir is envisaged in the future of music education [in that country]:

> In line with its practical approach, the college utilizes its limited resources to concentrate upon instrumental, rather than academic, musical education. Students above Grade V Royal Schools [ABRSM] standard receive a one-hour instrumental lesson per week, while those students who fall below this grade receive 45 minutes tuition per week. Clarinet students are encouraged to join the wind band, which constitutes some 40 players, at present 10 are clarinettists. The better clarinet students also have the opportunity to play in the College Symphony Orchestra, and if Bourdillon is able to realize one of his dreams (and enough Eb and bass clarinets can be found – Zimbabwe has just one bass clarinet in the whole country!), students may have the chance to play in a clarinet choir in future.[74]

The author has certainly identified signs of a clarinet choir movement in Australia. The Australian Clarinet and Saxophone Society were able to supply several addresses of clarinet choir directors who provided more detailed

---

[73] Correspondence between Fanie Jooste and the author from 16.10.2001, in which he informed the editor that there had certainly been small calrinet ensembles in Bloemfontein and in Cape Town but these were more as a part of an education programme (Fanie Jooste is Professor of Musicology and a Bassoon teacher at the Potchefstroom University for Christian Higher Education, School of Music and bassoonist in Potchefstroom University Symphony Orchestra).

[74] cf. Spencer Pitfield, 'The Clarinet in Zimbabwe', in: *The Clarinet*, May/June 1996, p. 18.

information about the development of clarinet choirs in Australia. I was therefore able to expand my research to the USA, Europe, Asia and Australia.

A pioneer of the Clarinet Choir Movement, the late Harvey Hermann from the University of Illinois, conductor of the clarinet choir there for some 23 years (1964-87) was also involved in this study. His great experience in this sector flowed into the project and was of inestimable value.

Summary:

The development of the clarinet choir into an effective musical means of expression should be seen in the narrow context with the historical development of the instruments themselves. The technical developments made in the area of key mechanism enabled manufacturers to construct lower clarinets. As the so-called Harmonie instruments were developed, they were first accepted and adopted in American concert [wind] orchestras/bands. The Contrabass Clarinet[75] completed the clarinet choir's instrumentation at the start of the 20th Century. From this we can deduce that as soon as the clarinets had been accepted in the concert orchestras [bands], stand-alone ensembles started to form. Although these ensembles were initially still a part of the orchestral programme at colleges and universities in America, very soon clarinet choirs began to establish themselves in the American school system as equally worthy, stand-alone concert ensembles.

But the fact is that, to date, no definite instrumentation or size of scoring has crystallised. Moreover in the course of working on this study, it became clear that lots of works in the basic scoring for only five clarinets (3 B flats, Alto and Bass Clarinet) can be played [in a clarinet choir]. Composers, arrangers and publishers score in very different ways. How effective the clarinet choir may be as a medium for teaching, largely depends on which transcriptions and arrangements the conductor has in his repertoire. If decent enough literature is played by the ensemble, then the children and students can gain experience of the different styles and epochs of musical history. In

---

[75] As the orchestral movement in America received great financial support from the public, orchestra conductors and directors were able to acquire their lower clarinets; cf. also Ch. 1.

my research, it has become all too evident that for many young music pupils, the clarinet choir is often the only opportunity they have to get to know sophisticated music and different styles. As a result of this study we can assume that directors and conductors of clarinet choirs prefer to play good transcriptions and arrangements. A large number of members of ensembles are busy making arrangements of music for their own groups. The reason may be that many ensembles find there is simply too little original literature available. Although the author can state that excellent original literature is available particularly in the USA and also now increasingly in Europe. While this should encourage teachers and conductors particularly in Europe to set up new choirs, they also need to persuade composers to write them good original pieces. In the educational context, another factor of crucial importance to be considered is the ability of clarinet choirs to improve an ensemble's performance ability. The early clarinet ensemble of Poncelet, Bellison and De Jesu were formed fundamentally with this in mind.[76] A statement by David Hite elucidates this view:

> The literature is a by-product, for a while at least, to the greater importance of this opportunity to learn how to tune blend, match staccato, and to apply the skills related to inflection and expression.[77]

Norman Heim, one of the grandfathers of this movement, echoed Hite's statement in 1972 commenting that his clarinet choir at the University of Maryland only gave two concerts a year.[78]

---

[76] cf. Ch. 3, Early Clarinet Ensembles in the USA particularly Simeon Bellison.

[77] David Hite, Correspondence with Vernon J. Hockett from 17.3.1972, in: *The Role of the Clarinet Choir as a Performance Ensemble*, loc.cit. p. 29.

[78] cf. V. Hockett, loc.cit. p. 92.

From the start, this stream of educational reflections seems to suggest that setting up new clarinet choirs was actually more important especially in the USA. Another considerable advantage of making music in a clarinet choir is that all members of the clarinet family are notated in treble or G clef and have almost the same tessitura (at least theoretically). This also makes it easy for the musician to change to another size of clarinet (not least because the instruments have by and large the same fingering system). In this research it has also become clear that the E flat clarinet is now fundamental to the tonal colour [of the clarinet choir] and should be required by all conductors. It is also essential for the conductor/leader to know that the 1st B flat clarinet part is not doubled [by the E flat] (otherwise [the E flat] is largely redundant). As far as the role of the basset horn is concerned, we can state than at least in America, Australia and Japan, it is hardly used. In Europe however, the basset horn is often preferred to the Alto Clarinet. This author also believes that for tuning and sound within the clarinet choir, the basset horn often works better than the Alto Clarinet.

The future success of clarinet choirs – viewed as a stand-alone concert ensemble - won't just depend on whether composers write original literature of sufficient quality and have it published. Certainly the pedagogical value of the ensemble is undisputed and this should contribute positively to its further development, particularly in establishing clarinet ensembles as concert choirs.

1.5   The Clarinet Choir – Development since 2005

Much has changed since I completed my research and my dissertation[79] on the clarinet choir.

As we have heard, the first clarinet choirs came into being in the 1950s as a project ensemble on many of the music camps in the USA. We should especially mention Professors Russell Howland, James De Jesu, Harold Palmer and Don McCathren as the pioneers of the clarinet choir.

After the 2nd World War, the work and experiments at the Music Camp in Hays, Kansas in the 50s represent the birth pangs of the first genuine clarinet choir.

Here I would like to mention the composer Alfred Reed who along with Don McCathren toured all across the USA helping to set up new clarinet choirs. Since the 1950s, the continuous development of instruments and the availability of the lower clarinets (Bass, E flat and B flat Contrabass clarinets) has of course been critically important for the rise and further development of the clarinet choir movement.

High school and college bands in turn were very keen to improve their clarinet sections. This encouraged the participation of many committed and experienced music teachers in founding clarinet choirs who significantly contributed to their establishment and spread.[80]

While the many pioneering clarinet 'clinics' were influential in the spread and development of clarinet choirs among other things in the 50s, in the

---

[79] Friedrich Pfatschbacher, *The Clarinet Choir* [Der Klarinettenchor], Universität Graz, Graz 2004 (Publ by Dr. Hans Schneider Verlag, 2005).
[80] cf. Ch 1.3.

60s, the role of promulgating this new form of musical ensemble was taken up by high school and college clarinet choirs. Over and above this, clarinet choir 'clinics' continued to be organised and this new type of ensemble encouraged the interest of such well-known composers as Gordon Jacob and Vaclav Nelhybel.

To foster more interest in composing for clarinet choirs, the first Composition Competition was promoted in the 1970s by the music publishers Kendor Music Inc in collaboration with the University of Maryland.

In more recent decades, the clarinet choir has seen more permanent developments through the addition and fuller integration of the lower clarinets (Bass and Contrabass Clarinets). Its larger range and huge tonal potential ultimately contributed to the triumph of this versatile form. In the last 40 years, professional ensembles have grown up not just in the USA but since the 80s in Europe, Australia and Japan.

Many larger scale works scored for modern large clarinet choirs are available in Europe from Belgian publishers. In this connection, it is worth singling out the Belgian clarinet choir Claribel[81] and the wonderful arrangements by Guido Six.[82] Many of his arrangements have been published by Andel Music[83] and they sometimes include separate parts for E flat, 1-4 B flat Clarinets, 2 E flat Alto Clarinets, 2 Bass, 1 E flat Contra-Alto and 1 B flat Contrabass Clarinet.

---

[81] cf. www.sixbros.com/claribel/ [accessed 27.2.2017]

[82] The founder and arranger of this Ensemble, Guido Six, was tragically killed along with his son Jef in a car accident in 2015. Since 2015 Claribel has been directed by Bart Picquer und Henk Soenen.

[83] cf. www.andelmusic.be [accessed 23.02.2017]

I should mention at this point that the quality of clarinet choir arrangements has certainly improved in the last 10-15 years. These days, recognised arrangers and composers are active as arrangers for clarinet choir. In Armin Suppan, the Austrian Clarinet Choir has a distinguished arranger within its own ranks. Many of his excellent arrangements and transcriptions have been published by Kliment.[84] And the composer and arranger Theodor Demmel also often writes for our clarinet choir.

Very fine arrangements and original material are available in England[85] and the USA. In the States there are innumerable publishers that one could mention here, which would run to several pages. So I would like instead to draw attention to a feature and list by Margaret Thornhill[86] that has appeared regularly over a number of years in 'The Clarinet Choir' in the international trade periodical *The Clarinet*. (This first appeared in September 2007.) In her column, Thornhill mainly researches worldwide into extraordinary clarinet choirs and contributes interviews, current developments, repertoire suggestions etc.

These days clarinet choirs have also established themselves as concert ensembles on the concert platforms of Europe, Japan, Australia and also in South America not just in the USA.

---

[84] cf. www.andelmusic.be [accessed 23.02.2017]
[85] cf. www.cassgb.org/library/ [accessed 23.02.2017]
[86] cf. Magaret Thornhill, 'The Clarinet Choir', in: *The Clarinet*, Vol. 34, No. 4, September 2007 ff.

The Clarinet Choir Scene in Austria

As this form of ensemble only established itself for individual projects, as an example of the clarinet choir movement in Austria, I would like to examine more closely the Austrian Clarinet Choir which has become a firm part of the Austrian cultural scene in the last 10 years.

Austrian Clarinet Choir (Österreichischer Klarinettenchor)

The Clarinet Choir of the the Austrian Clarinet Society (ACS) was founded in 2007 at the 1st International Clarinet Congress in Mautern by Friedrich Pfatschbacher. This ensemble consists of students, teachers and committed amateur musicians who come together from across Austria for projects. In the Austrian Clarinet Choir (ACC), it soon became clear that the tone colour of the E flat clarinet is indispensable so now the author tends not to programme many works without E flat clarinet. At the same time it is also vital that this instrument does not simply double the 1st clarinet part.

The basset horn is used more often in clarinet choirs in Europe than it is in America, Japan or Australia where it seldom makes an appearance. In the author's opinion the basset horn's soft and sonorous sound and intonation blends with the clarinet choir rather better than the Alto Clarinet's often harsher sound.

These days, some modern compositions or arrangements available on the market don't readily suit the Clarinet Choir. It is simply not good enough for example, to take a string ensemble arrangement and thoughtlessly transpose it for Clarinet Choir without thinking about the voice leading. Musicians will always point out that such compositions or arrangements are either unbalanced or lack 'body' in the sound. This may have something to do with the [odd-numbered] overtones of the clarinet. In arrangements, care needs to be taken that the distance between voices is not greater than an octave.

Good compositions or arrangements should have balanced voice leading and with regard to the sound of the Choir, they should aim for a rather mellow and rounded sound. [In my opinion] when trying to produce a compact and homogeneous sound, it is crucial to consider the scoring.

The preferred scoring of the ACC with around 30 musicians is:

1 E flat, 4 x 5 B flat Clarinets (1-4), 2 Basset horns, 2 Alto Clarinets, 2-3 Bass Clarinets, 2 Contra-Alto Clarinets, 1 Contrabass Clarinet

Having a Contrabass Clarinet will help to produce a really rounded and homogeneous sound.

My work with the Austrian Clarinet Choir has also demonstrated that the clarinet choir is often the only opportunity for many young school musicians to get to know worthwhile literature and different styles.

The ACC's repertoire covers all periods of music history with special emphasis on Romantic and 20th Century music. The ensemble always enjoys playing new original contemporary works.[87] As the public also really enjoys works for solo voice and clarinet choir, these are often included in the ACC's programmes.

---

[87] Here I would like to mention the many excellent arrangements and adaptations by Armin Suppan, available from the publishers Kliment Verlag and also draw attention of the reader the compositions by Franz Cibulka (d. 2016).

Plate 3: ACC at the Clarinetfest in Madrid 2015

Other noteworthy clarinet choirs and firmly established occasional ensembles in Austria include:

Tirol Clarinet Orchestra

The Clarinet Orchestra of Innsbruck City Musikschule was founded in 1987 by Peter Rabl. As a result of opportunities and experiences over the years, he is now able to call upon a large ensemble of up to 30 musicians. The members are current and former pupils of the Innsbruck Music School, often supplemented by teachers in concerts and recordings.[88]

Vienna Clarinet Orchestra

The Vienna Clarinet Orchestra was founded in 1993 on the initiative of Prof Kurt Schmid and is the only one of its kind in the capital. Set up along the lines of the Tokyo Clarinet Choir, this Ensemble comprises mostly amateur musicians and is currently conducted by Reinhold Nowotny.[89]

Pinzgau Clarinet Choir (Salzburg)

The Pinzgau Clarinet Choir was founded from current clarinet teachers in 2007 as a community project primarily in Pinzgau (Salzburg) with financial support from the Pinzgau Wind Music Association. The target groups and members are personnel in the clarinet sections of all the Wind Bands in Pinzgau from whom an ensemble was formed so that they can develop their playing by performing artistically and technically challenging works in a more open formation than is common in wind music.[90]

---

[88] cf. www.innsbruck.gv.at [accessed on 22.05.2017]
[89] cf. www.klarinettenorchester.at [accessed on 22.05.2017]
[90] cf. www.musikum-salzburg.at [accessed on 22.05.2017]

2 The Stylistic Development of Repertoire for Clarinet Choir

2.1 Instrumentation, Scoring and Tonal Options

As we heard in the last chapter, there are many factors involved in the development of the Clarinet Choir. Looking at its tonal options, we should view the various Clarinets' own registers - Soprano, Alto, Tenor and Bass down to the Contrabass Clarinet - as akin to the string registers within the symphony orchestra. The parallel with string registers is not only appreciable in the clarinet's ability to play technical and lyrical pas-sages, but also particularly evident in the clarinet register's timbre and variety of tonal colours. Furthermore, as they were often coupled with the [lower] saxophones in the early part of the 20th Century, this suggests that the Alto and Bass Clarinets hadn't assume their proper place in the clarinet section.[91]

The development of the clarinet choir within the context of the American Concert Band therefore played a particularly crucial role in developing its instrumentation, not least because experiments by leading composers, conductors and arrangers were just as decisive for the clarinet family's function within the concert band, as they were for its development as a stand-alone ensemble.

Some of these individuals include among others James R. Gillette, Austin Harding, Donald McCathren, Alfred Reed, William D. Revelli, Lucien Cailliet and John Redfield. So let us take a closer look at the individual

---

[91] cf. F. J. Cipolla, D. Hunsberger (Ed.), loc.cit. p. 116.

contribution of these trail-blazers in the development of a standard in-strumentation for clarinet choir.

James R. Gillette

Gillette was born in Rosebloom, NY on 30th May 1886 and died on 26th November 1963 in Lake Forest, Illinois. After completing his musical studies at the University of Syracuse, he took over the direction of the Carleton College Symphonic Band (Minnesota).[92] Gillette became well-known in the area of instrumentation. Among other things, he arranged the Symphony in B flat (1926) by Paul R. M. Fauchet. He also contributed many articles to the trade magazine *School Music* in 1930 about his ideas and the role of the clarinet within the American Concert Band. He vigorously expressed the opinion that a [Wind] Orchestra doesn't need particularly large forces to be really good. Gillette's suggestion for a 50 man ensemble is as follows:[93]

---

[92] Wolfgang & Armin Suppan, loc.cit. p. 274.
[93] George D. Stirrat, loc.cit. p. 64.

Table 6: Gillette's Scoring List for a 50 piece [Wind] Orchestra

1st & 2nd Flutes	2		1st & 2nd Trumpets	2
1st & 2nd Oboes	2		3rd & 4th Trumpets	2
E flat Clarinet	1		1st & 2nd Trumpets	2
1st B flat Clarinets	8		3rd & 4th Horns	2
2nd B flat Clarinets	8		1st & 2nd Trombones	2
Alto Clarinet	1		Bass Trombone	1
Bass Clarinet	1		Baritone	1
B flat Soprano Saxophone	1		Celli	3
Alto Saxophone	1		Double Bass	2
Tenor Saxophone	1		Tuba	1
Baritone Saxophone	1		Timpani	1 pair
Bass Saxophone or Sarrusophone	1		Percussion (drums)	2
			Total	**50**

As we can see, there is no Contrabass Clarinet in Gillette's Ensemble[94] although it does appear in the same year 1930 in the scoring list of the University of Illinois (see Chapter 1 Development of the Clarinet Choir). Gillette advocated that the clarinets within the American Concert Band were

---

[94] This article was published in the Jan/Feb 1930 edition of the trade magazine *School Music.*

the equivalent to the violins of a symphony orchestra and effectively a type of 'basic choir'. This corroborates the following statement:

> As the string quartet is the foundation of the orchestra, so it would be of value for composers and arrangers to experiment in the writing of quartets and quintets for B-flat, alto, and bass clarinets.[95]

Gillette used Alto and Bass Clarinets in three ways:

1. as Tenor and Bass especially in Clarinet Quartets
2. in unison or octaves with the B flat clarinets and
3. as solo instruments particularly to achieve special effects.[96]

Gillette was one of the first to advocate the use of the clarinets inside the American Concert Band as a type of 'basic choir' sonority. But following his scoring suggestion, it is difficult to imagine that a balanced sound could be achieved within the choir with a single Alto and Bass Clarinet to 16 clarinets.

Albert Austin Harding

Harding is considered to be one of the pioneers of the 'school band movement'. Born on 10th February 1880 in Georgetown, Illinois, Harding directed the famous University of Illinois band from 1907-1948 and made a name for himself mainly in the area of orchestral instrumentation.[97] He died on 3rd December 1958. As well as his experiments with rarer and 'exotic'

---

[95] James R. Gillette, 'Woodwinds and the Symphonie band', in: *School Music*, Vol. 30, Mar-Apr 1930, p. 26.
[96] Ibid. p. 26.
[97] A. Austin Harding Collection [http.//gateway.library.uiuc.edu/sousa/aah-bio.htm, accessed 23.08.2002].

instruments, he was among the first to adopt the complete Sarrusophone family into the [Wind] Orchestra in 1924. By scoring the Illinois [Wind] Orchestra with a generally larger number of wind instruments, he solved the 'brass heavy' concept of the American band. Influenced by his friend, Sousa, Harding believed that in the area of technical and performance ability, wind orchestras should aspire to the same standards expected of symphony orchestras.

> He sought to give the Illinois band a symphonic sound by making greater use of oboes, bassoons, alto and bass flutes and clarinets, the full saxophone family, flugelhorns, horns instead of altos, and a contrabassoon.[98]

As previously mentioned in Chapter 1, Harding was the first to score for Alto and Bass Clarinet in a University wind orchestra. Alto and Bass Clarinets were introduced in 1906 and 1907 respectively. Only in 1930 did the Contrabass Clarinet appear for the first time in the line up of the Illinois Band. Sources suggest no previous use of a Contrabass Clarinet in an American [Wind] Orchestra. In assessing the development of the clarinet choir within the Illinois Band, Harding's efforts and experiments in instrumentation were decisive in later establishing the clarinet choir as a 'stand alone' ensemble. That Alto, Bass and Contrabass Clarinets were accepted in an American Wind Orchestra was largely due to his commitment.[99]

---

[98] Raoul F. Camus, Art. 'Bands', in: The New Grove Dictionary of American Music, Vol. 1, ed. H. W. Hitchcock and S. Sadie, London 1986, pp. 127-137; cf. Achim Hofer, *Blasmusikforschung. Eine kritische Einführung*, [Wind Music Research a critical introduction] Darmstadt, 1952, p. 225.
[99] cf. George D. Stirrat, loc.cit. p. 67-68.

Alfred Reed und Donald McCathren

Very early on, the American composer Alfred Reed showed serious interest in the clarinet choir. Initially, Reed recognised the use of the clarinet choir as the 'basic choir' within the 'American Concert Band'. Like Gillette, Reed also made several suggestions for an effective standard instrumentation for concert band later to be influential across the USA. Also agreeing with Gillette, Reed firmly believed that the Clarinet Choir fulfilled the same role/function as the string section in a symphony orchestra.[100] One can therefore also conclude that [in the band] the lower brass instruments no longer needed to double the Bass and Contrabass registers of the Clarinet Choir. Of course the instrumentation of individual works varies considerably and depends largely on the structure of the work and the composer or arranger's imagination, as Reed wrote in a letter to the author:

> The instrumentation varies according to the nature of the piece they are performing and who the composer or arranger may have been, and what he called for in his score. In my own works, whether for clarinet choir alone or as the basic component of the wind orchestra, I always score for, I call for 18 players, as follows: 1 Eb Soprano Clarinet, 12 Bb Soprano Clarinets (usually 4 first, 4 second and 4 third), 2 Eb Alto, 2 Bb Bass, and 1 Bb Contrabass ...[101]

As the above quotation reveals, Alfred Reed made no distinction in the clarinet choir's instrumentation whether used in the wind Orchestra or as a

---

[100] cf. George D. Stirrat, loc.cit. p. 69.
[101] Reed Alfred: Correspondence with the author from 25th August 2002.

'stand alone' [clarinet] ensemble. This in turn reflects the parallel development of the clarinet choir as an individual ensemble alongside [its role in] the American Concert Band.

As mentioned in Chapter 3, in his pioneering work with the Clarinet Choir, Alfred Reed was supported and accompanied on several trips by Don McCathren Orchestral Director of Duquesne University. When McCathren formed and directed the Symphonie of Winds in 1964, he put Reed's ideas into practice. McCathren wrote about his orchestra in an article in 1966:

> The instrumentation consists of a large clarinet choir and one on a part throughout the rest of the instrumentation. Having one player perform on each part gives brilliance, clarity and greater colour contrasts, just as achieved in orchestral scoring.[102]

Lucien Cailliet

Cailliet was born on 22nd May 1891 in Châlon-sur-Marne and died on 27th December 1984 in California. During his military service in Dijon, he studied at the Paris Conservatoire. After his diploma in 1913, he entered upon a career path as a military band leader or kapellmeister. In 1915 he gave concerts with this wind orchestra in the USA and as the States fascinated him, he decided to settle there. From 1919 to 1938 he was a member of Stokowsky's Philadephia Orchestra both as a clarinettist and arranger. He taught at the Curtis Institute attaining his doctorate in 1937 at the Philadelphia Music Academy. In 1938 he was appointed Professor of Orches-

---

[102] Don E. McCathren, 'The New Sound - The Symphonie of Winds', in: *The School Musician*, Vol. 38, Oct 1966, ibid.

tration, Counterpoint and Conducting at the University of Southern California. From 1945-57 he toured as a Guest Conductor and wrote the music to 25 films. In 1957 he took up the appointment of Music Director of the Leblanc Corporation. He retired in 1976.[103]

When the then Bass Clarinettist of the New York Symphony, a Mr. Parme, brought the first Contrabass Clarinet made by Buffet to the States, Cailliet played this instrument as a member of the Philadelphia Orchestra. Even the conductor Leopold Stokowsky, who was particularly fond of experimenting with instrumentation, was drawn to this new instrument. Cailliet became America's leading orchestral arranger and more importantly here, a firm advocate of the Clarinet Choir within the Concert Band. Acting with considerable personal initiative, Lucien Cailliet was determined to demonstrate the advantages of the Clarinet Choir for the Wind Orchestra and he set about promoting this on his concert tours. Many Clarinet Choir works by Cailliet belong to current standard repertoire (for example: *Caprice Sentimental, Carnaval, Poem & Fantasie* - all of which appeared in Leblanc's catalogue). Cailliet's scoring suggestion for an optimal and balanced sound is identical to the mixed choir: Soprano, Alto, Tenor and Bass. In this layout, Cailliet specifies that the Clarinet Choir's function was as a 'basic choir'. Based on the above mentioned layout his proposed scoring is as follows:[104]

[103] Wolfgang & Armin Suppan, loc.cit. p. 170.
[104] cf. George D. Stirrat, loc.cit. pp. 71-72; cf. also Lucien Cailliet, *The Clarinet and Clarinet Choir*, Wisconsin 1955.

Table 7: Lucien Cailliet's Scoring suggestion

Soprano	2 E flat Clarinets, 6 1st Clarinets, 5 2nds, 5 3rds
Alto	4 Alto Clarinets
Tenor	4 Bass Clarinets
Bass	2 Contrabass Clarinets

The author considers that Lucien Cailliet's scoring above is nicely balanced and this is as valid for the stand alone Clarinet Choir as for the clarinet section within the American Concert Band.

William D. Revelli and John Redfield

William Donald Revelli was born on 12th February 1902 in Spring Gulch, Colorado and died in 1994. He started with violin lessons aged 5 as a pupil of Dominic Sarli. Graduating from Chicago Musical College in 1922, he continued his pedagogical education at the Columbia School of Music in Chicago, receiving his teaching diploma in 1925. In 1935 he became Director of the University of Michigan Band in Ann Arbor. With his symphonic [wind] orchestra he made many trips abroad (including a 16 week tour in 1961). In 1971 Revelli became Emeritus Director of the University of Michigan [Wind] Orchestra. As Director and a firm advocate of bands within the US school system, he continued the tradition of P. Fillmore and Albert Austin Harding.[105]

---

[105] Nicolas Slonimsky/Laura Kuhn (Ed.), *Baker's Biographical Dictionary of Musicians*, New York, 2001, p. 2970.

William Revelli wanted to establish his concert band as a serious orchestra. Already in early 1952 he wrote the following:

> [...] if we are to restrict the use of the alto, bass and contrabass clarinets to such an extent that these instruments are either non-existent or used in such meagre numbers that they fail to contribute effectively to the general performance, then our bands will remain static, and limited in tonal colour and flexibility.[106]

Revelli's suggestion for the 'balanced clarinet choir' accords with Alfred Reed's comparison with the string section in the symphony orchestra. To balance 16 B flat clarinets, he suggested 4 Altos, 4 Basses and 3 Contras. For 20 B flats, he proposed 4 Alto, 4 Basses and 2 Contrabasses but to balance 24 B flat clarinets he reckoned on no fewer than 8 Altos, 8 Basses and 4 Contras! Revelli envisaged the scoring of Alto and Bass Clarinets in exact proportion to the number of B flat Clarinets:

> [...] the number of alto and bass clarinets should be equal and should increase by two as the B-flat soprano clarinets are increased by four. The contrabass clarinets should be one-half the number of alto or bass clarinets.[107]

Revelli's determined efforts to establish the Clarinet Choir as a 'basic choir' within the American Concert [Wind] Orchestra were very significant for the development of the Clarinet Choir particularly in the 1960s.

---

[106] cf. George D. Stirrat, loc.cit. p. 73
[107] cf. William D. Revelli, 'The Balanced Clarinet Choir' in: *The Instrumentalist*, Vol. 7, Nov-Dec, 1952, pp. 14-15.

The problems of orchestral instrumentation were pointed out scientifically by John Redfield, Professor of Physics at Columbia University in his book *Music Science and an Art* (Tudor Publishing Company, NY, 1928):

> It is as lacking in balance as would be a symphony orchestra having first and second violins and brass only.[108]

Like Revelli and Reed, Redfield also believed that the clarinet family should possess the same balance and function as the strings in a symphony orchestra:

> What should be done, of course, is to include alto, bass and contrabass clarinets in the band in about the same rations that the violas, `cellos, and string basses bear to the violins of the orchestra. The clarinet choir should posses the same balance between its soprano, alto, tenor, bass and contrabass voices, as does the string choir of the orchestra. Without this tonal balance in the band's principal choir can be no symphonie band; with it there can.[109]

To attain this balance in a concert band, as he mentions above, Redfield suggested the following scoring along the same lines as the string section:

> 12 1st B flat Clarinets, 12 2nd B flat Clarinets, 8 Basset horns or E flat Alto Clarinets, 8 Bass Clarinets and 6 E flat Contra Alto Clarinets.[110]

Of the different organisations that helped in developing an original repertoire and a standardised instrumentation for the concert band, two stand out: the American Bandmaster Association (ABA) founded in 1929, and the

---

[108] John Redfield, *Music. A Science and an Art*, New York 1928, S. 299.

[109] ibid, p. 299.

[110] ibid, p. 300.

College Band Directors National Association (CBDNA) set up in 1941 by William D.Revelli. Among other things this organisation awarded commissions for new works for original wind music to such established composers well-known in other genres of music, including Ernst Krenek [the German-American] and [the Argentinian-American composer] Mario Davidovsky.[111]

So the evidence seems to demonstrate that the emancipation of the clarinet choir within the American Concert Band was very important for the emergence of the Clarinet choir as a stand alone ensemble. But it was only in the 1960s, mainly through the commitment of Russell Howland and James De Jesu[112] and many other arrangers, that an effective standardised instrumentation began to evolve as follows:

> E flat Clarinet, 1nd, 2nd, 3rd Clarinets in B flat Alto Clarinet in E flat, Bass Clarinet in B flat, Contrabass Clarinet (in B flat or Contra Alto in E flat)[113]

In combining clarinets in a choir, each new voice contributes an important function. If we compare the Clarinet Choir with the string ensemble, we also see the same flexibility. To achieve a really balanced and homogeneous sound, the size and the scoring of the Choir is relevant. In his 1968 essay,

---

[111] R. F. Camus, Art. 'Bands', in: *The New Grove Dictionary of American Music*, Vol. 1, ed. H. W. Hitchcock and S. Sadie, London 1986, pp. 127-137.
[112] cf. Ch 1 'The Development of the Clarinet Choir'.
[113] Excerpt by the author; cf. also N. Heim, loc.cit. pp. 109-120.

The Clarinet Choir of Yesterday and Today Richard K. Weerts[114] wrote about the scoring for clarinet choir:

> The clarinet choir, in its most basic form, can consist of three B flat, one alto, and one bass clarinet. This combination can be expanded to a more fully balanced choir comprised of 3 x 1st B flat clarinets (one doubles on E flat soprano clarinet), 3 x 2nd B flat clarinets, 3 x 3rd B flat clarinets, 3 Alto clarinets, 3 Bass clarinets, 1 E flat Contra-Alto clarinet and 1 B flat Contrabass clarinet.[115]

To achieve a really homogeneous and symphonic sound, the E flat Soprano and Contrabass part (sometimes given to the Contra-Alto) should definitely be included. The E flat should ideally have its own part and not double the 1st Clarinet Part. Even the 2 Contrabass voices should be afforded separate parts and should never merely double the Bass Clarinet.

As far as the A flat Sopranino and the Basset horn are concerned, parts for these instruments are often included as optional by some composers.[116]

Lucien Cailliet, one of the greatest arrangers for Clarinet Choir, liked scoring for the A flat Sopranino (sounding in the same register as the piccolo), the basset horn and Contra-Alto in E flat thereby covering a tonal range of

---

[114] Richard K. Weerts was Professor of music and chairman of the Instrumental Music Committee at Northeast Missouri State College in Kirksville; cf. 'Biographies', in: Woodwind Anthology. A Compendium of Woodwind Articles from *The Instrumentalist* [Ed.], loc.cit. p. 1432.

[115] R. K. Weerts, loc.cit. p. 833.

[116] ibid, p. 833.

some 6 octaves. Had he scored for Sub-Contrabass Clarinet, he would have reached a range of 7½ octaves, larger than an orchestra![117]

Another advocate of the A flat Sopranino was the Clarinet Choir pioneer Harvey Hermann who founded and conducted the University of Illinois Clarinet Choir (1965-81). In 2004 he wrote to the author:

The complete Clarinet Choir from A flat Sopranino down to the B flat Contrabass spans the entire range of the piano keyboard. Giving the Ensemble great flexibility of range and a wide range of volume in all Registers.[118]

Whereas John Morgan mentioned in his Diploma thesis in the 1960s that the E flat clarinet was largely considered optional,[119] these days, it is inconceivable to imagine compositions and arrangements without it. Only occasionally is the part considered optional and in most cases it is treated independently. When arranging for this very flexible instrument, it is very important to write for it idiomatically and to ensure that the technical passages are playable. Generally this very demanding part should be played by an experienced E flat player, otherwise there is cer-tainly a danger of encountering insuperable difficulties with intonation.

Scoring for Alto Clarinet shouldn't be a cause for concern these days. The instrument crops up in all sorts of arrangements and original compositions. This goes back partly to the fact that the 'basic choir' of clarinets had established itself in the 1950s and 60s in the American Concert [Wind]

---

[117] cf. G. D. Stirrat, loc.cit. pp. 71–72.
[118] Harvey Herman: Correspondence (questionnaire) with the Author from 29.02.2004.
[119] J. B. Morgan, loc.cit. p. 52.

Orchestra.[120] Norman Rost another of the Clarinet Choir pioneers writes about scoring for the Alto clarinet:

> I am convinced, however, that the alto clarinet provides a definite colour which can be most valuable if used correctly. In fact, the clarinet choir and quartet cannot be complete without this instrument… The placing of the alto clarinet on the third part eliminates the need for unnatural adjustments since the part falls a fifth higher on the instrument, placing it in a more brilliant register, and since the tonal colour blends better in that voice than does the soprano clarinet.[121]

In this context we can confirm that scoring for Alto Clarinet gives the Clarinet Choir a greater balance and its more varied range of tonal colour generally enhances the choir's tone quality.

At this point it is worth mentioning the scoring list of the International Clarinet Choir Festival in Mid-Europe in 1999 artistically directed by Eugen Brixel and Franz Cibulka, where a work by Cibulka was premiered in a version for clarinet choir. His work Clariphonic was scored for:

> 1 E flat Clarinet, 16 B flat Clarinets, 1 Basset Horn, 1 Alto Clarinet, 3 Bass Clarinets, 1 Contra-Alto Clarinet, 1 Contrabass

The group Vienna Clarinet Connection also took part in this premiere providing 2 B flat clarinets, 2 basset horns and a bass clarinet.[122]

Norman Heim's articles offer a very good overview about scoring and set up of a clarinet choir. Generally he refers the size of a clarinet choir to a

---

[120] cf. W. D. Revelli, *The Balanced Clarinet Choir*, loc.cit. pp. 14-15.

[121] cf. N. Rost, 'Place of the Alto Clarinet in the Clarinet Choir', in: *The Instrumentalist*, Vol. 13, Mar. 1954, p. 34.

[122] The Author took part in this concert on 16.7.1999.

chamber music scoring with one to a part or comprising the following scoring:

> 1 E flat Clarinet, 2-3 on each of the 3 B flat Clarinet parts, 1 Alto Clarinet, 1 Bass Clarinet, 1 Contrabass if available

Large formations of ca. 30-50 players, writes Heim, are often unusual and to be found only in a couple of American Universities (for instance Lebanon Valley College [Pennsylvania]).[123]

In assigning more to a part, one has to be very careful to give enough attention to a homogeneous sound.

In his article on the subject of tonal practice, Johann Mösenbichler comments:

> From a physical standpoint, the division of parts within a multi-part register is of critical importance for the overall sound.[124]

It is fundamentally important not to over-score the first parts and the Contrabass parts in contrast to the middle voices, i.e. the 2nd, 3rd Clarinets in B flat, Alto and Bass Clarinets.

Mösenbichler continues about the distribution of parts in a wind orchestra:

> Only an intelligent and balanced division of parts within a register can create the precondition for a physically sound tonal basis.[125]

---

[123] cf. N. Heim, loc.cit. p. 112.

[124] cf. J. Mösenbichler, ‚Intelligente Sitzordnung. Überlegungen und Erfahrungen zum Thema Klangarbeit' [Intelligent Seating Plan, Considerations and Experiences on the subject of Sound Rehearsals] (2), in: Clarino.print, Vol. 2, Book 2, Feb 2004, p. 14.

[125] ibid.

Here is an example of scoring from the All Eastern High School Choir from 1979:

> 1 E flat Clarinet, 8 x 1st B flat Clarinets, 9 x 2nd B flat Clarinets, 11 x 3rd B flat Clarinets, 10 Alto Clarinets, 6 Bass Clarinets, 4 E flat Contra-Alto Clarinets[126]

Quite how large the scoring of a clarinet choir should be depends of course on the piece to be played. This is supported by Thomas A. Ayres:

> In speaking of the clarinet choir, I refer to any ensemble of clarinets numbering five or more, at least one of which is of bass range. One of the points I wish to emphasize most strongly is that, in my opinion, there is no instrumentation for all clarinet choirs. The best instrumentation largely depends upon the work to be played.[127]

Although there has been an effective standard instrumentation since the 1960s, as already mentioned, the basset horn can generally support the alto clarinet and thereby contribute to a more homogeneous sound. Norman Heim believes the reason for this is that the Basset sounds similar in the *clarino* and *altissimo* registers. If it is not possible to score for the basset horn, a fuller sound can be produced in all three registers when using the alto clarinet by widening the tone chamber of the mouthpiece and using E flat alto saxophone reeds.[128]

Whether to include a contra-alto in E flat or a contrabass clarinet in B flat is a matter for the artistic director to decide. It is worth pointing out that at

---

[126] cf. N. Heim, 'The Clarinet Choir Phenomenon', in: Woodwind Anthology, A compendium of Woodwind Articles from *The Instrumentalist*, Vol. 2, p. 952.

[127] cf. Thomas A. Ayres, 'Arranging for the Clarinet Choir', in: *The Instrumentalist*, Vol. 11, Jan 1957, p. 26.

[128] N. Heim, loc.cit. p. 952.

least in the USA, where the Clarinet Choir has its roots, the contra-alto certainly seems to have prevailed. As Thomas Ayres pointed out in exploring this, the contra-alto is technically more flexible and has more resonance tones than the contrabass in B flat. Another factor is that the lower notes of the contrabass in B flat have strong 3rd and 5th partials and therefore the fundamental is not so audible. Whatever the preference, the most important thing is to include at least one contrabass instrument.[129]

In this context, Norman Heim mentioned that the contra-alto can be serviced more easily and it is worth considering that it generally needs fewer repairs.[130] For larger clarinet choir works these days you would expect parts for both instruments to be available. So the complete tonal spectrum of the contrabass should be exploited when arranging or composing for clarinet choir.

In the context of the reception of pieces, the lay out of the ensemble plays an huge role. The tonal experience can be thoroughly influenced by this. Two factors are critical:

1. The seating arrangement should be chosen that ensures the work to be performed can be played with the best tonal balance.

2. The composition or arrangement should be suitable for clarinet choir.

As sound is always concerned with tension and release, this is very much the same situation as the sound of an orchestra. The sound of the clarinet choir

---

[129] T. Ayres, loc.cit. p. 26.
[130] N. Heim, loc.cit. p. 952.

doesn't just result from the purely instrumental sound but it includes the parameters of balance and dynamics.[131]

The main consideration in seating arrangements results from the fact that the listener experiences the performance from different angles.

So each listener experiences their own individual version of the ensemble's sound. In most cases, the audience sits directly in front of the group. The orchestra does have the chance to specify the direction of sound perceived by the listener. So the seating arrangement of the clarinet choir should be determined so that, as far as possible, every member of the audience experiences the best tonal presence.

In principle though there is no optimal seating plan as every concert hall acoustic is different. Other factors are also worth considering, for example the size of the stage that may not allow for the best lay out. It is then necessary to adapt the ensemble's seating plan according to the given circumstances.

Before deciding on a seating plan it is important to establish the size of the ensemble. With careful planning the conductor can compensate for weaker registers so that they balance with the rest of the ensemble.

The author recommends in this regard that the E flat clarinet and contrabass are not doubled, as these instruments play solo parts.[132] Although there are certainly some disproportionately large choirs who do double these parts, it is worth pointing out here that over-large clarinet choirs do not always make

---

[131] cf. J. Mösenbichler, ‚Der gute Ton macht die Musik. Überlegungen und Erfahrungen zum Thema Klangarbeit' [Good Sound creates Music. Considerations and Experiences on the Subject of Sound Rehearsals] (1), in: *Clarino.print*, Vol. 2, Book 1, Feb 2004, p. 19.
[132] The problem of instrumentation was discussed at the beginning of the chapter.

for the best sound. When considering seating arrangements and acoustic, the conductor should choose the best possible instrumental lay out after considering all important factors.

To assist conductors, here are some interesting, tried and tested seating arrangements recommended by distinguished conductors and professors with many years experience of conducting clarinet choirs.[133]

William H. Stubbins former clarinet professor at the University of Michigan and a clarinet choir pioneer suggests three seating plans of different sizes.[134]

---

[133] cf. J. Morgan, loc.cit. p. 60 ff.

[134] W. H. Stubbins carried out various experiments in seating plans with his clarinet choir of students at the University of Michigan; cf. ibid.

1. Small Clarinet Choirs

This group comprises no more than 7 or 8 musicians.

2 1st B flat Clarinets, 2 2nd B flat Clarinets, 2 Altos and 1 or 2 Bass Clarinets

Where two Bass Clarinettists of equal merit are unavailable for such a group, it is not entirely necessary to double the Bass Clarinet part. According to Stubbins, there are two possible seating arrangements appropriate for the small choir. From experience, the so-called 'String Quartet' arrangement (see Diagram 1 or 2) seems the better choice for a small group of clarinet comprising:

This seating arrangement has two distinct advantages:

1. The Musicians who mostly play together, sit opposite each other – the sound focuses in the middle and doesn't get lost in the room.

2. The important parts of Alto and 3rd Clarinets are positioned on the outside.

A = 1st Clarinet, B = 2nd Clarinet, C = Alto or 3rd Clarinet, D = Bass Clarinet

Diagram 1: String Quartet Seating Plan

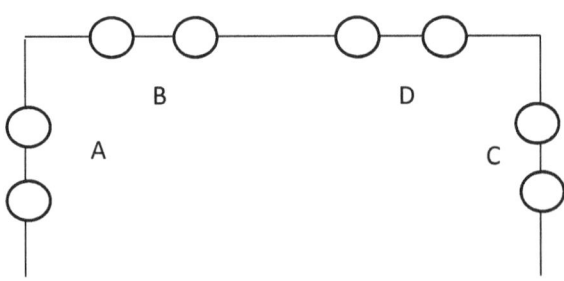

Stubbins' second seating suggestion is an orchestral set up. Here alto and bass clarinets are interchangeable without changing anything fundamental.

A = 1st Clarinet, B = 2nd Clarinet, C = Alto or 3rd Clarinet, D = Bass Clarinet

Diagram 2: String Quartet Seating Plan

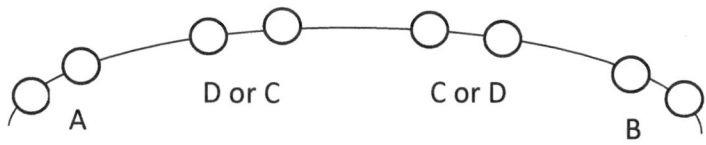

D or C   C or D

A   B

2. Medium sized Clarinet Choirs

The medium sized Clarinet Choir consists of the 8 musicians of the small choir plus a additional player of B flat and bass parts respectively. For this group at least 2 bass clarinets are required. New to this ensemble is the 3rd clarinet (3 of these) and if required also the E flat and contrabass clarinet. The best seating position for this group is in the form of a pyramid.

A = E flat Clarinet, B = 1st B flat Clarinet, C = 2nd B flat Clarinet,
D = Alto - or 3rd B flat Clarinet, E = Bass Clarinet, F = Contrabass Clarinet

Diagram 3: Pyramid Seating Plan

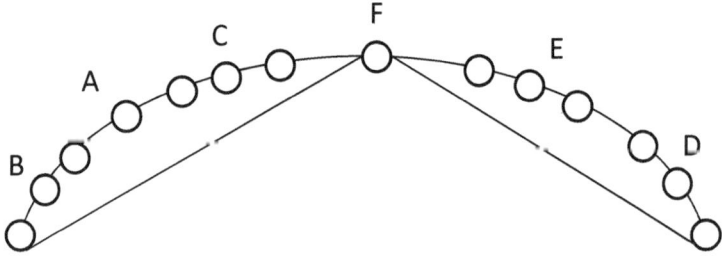

Don McCathren offers another option. Here the musicians are laid out in a semi-circle. The higher clarinets sit to the left of the conductor with the lower instruments arranged to the right.

Plate 4: Kansas All-State Music Camp Clarinet Choir[135]

---

[135] Photo shows Don McCathren with his Kansas All-State Music Camp Clarinet Choir in June 1955; cf. also J. Morgan, loc.cit. p. 63.

3. Large Clarinet Choirs

The ideal seating plan comprises an ensemble of

1 E flat Clarinet (if required), 4 x 1st, 2nd, 3rd & 4th B flat Clarinets (16 in all), 2 Alto Clarinets 2 Bass Clarinets and 2 Contrabass Clarinets

These days many choirs have larger formations but we also know that when using several players to a part the greatest care should be exercised in the context of sound quality and transparency. This sketch should clarify the seating plan:

A E flat Clarinet   E 4th B flat Clarinet

B 1st B flat Clarinet   F Alto Clarinet

C 2nd B flat Clarinet   G Bass Clarinet

D 3rd B flat Clarinet   H Contrabass clarinet

Diagram 4: Large Clarinet Choir

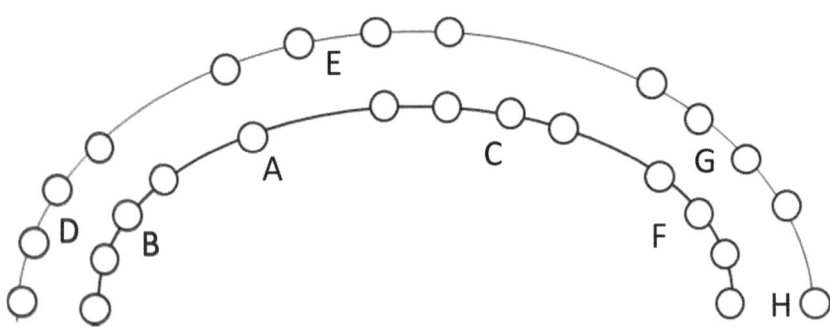

According to Norman Heim 2 seating plans have proved successful for nor-
mal sizes of a clarinet choir (12-15 members). For a concertante performance the seating plan in the form of a wind orchestra should be adopted:
for recordings 2 or 3 semi-circles have been crystalised. If the ensemble consists of 20-30 musicians, a wind instrument exhibition should be considered. For very large performances with around 100 musicians I recommend
a semi-circular seating plan in the form of a symphony orchestra.[136]

Diagram 5: Seating Plan for 16 Musicians

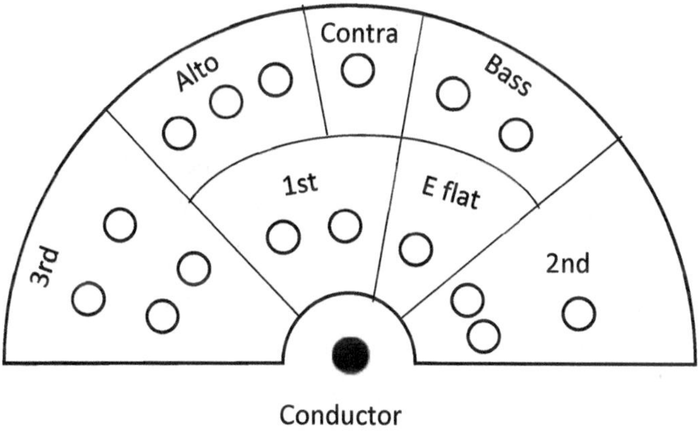

Conductor

---

[136] Norman Heim, loc.cit. p. 952; cf. also *The Development of the Clarinet Choir in the USA*, loc.cit. p. 109.

Diagram 6: Seating Plan for 49 Musicians

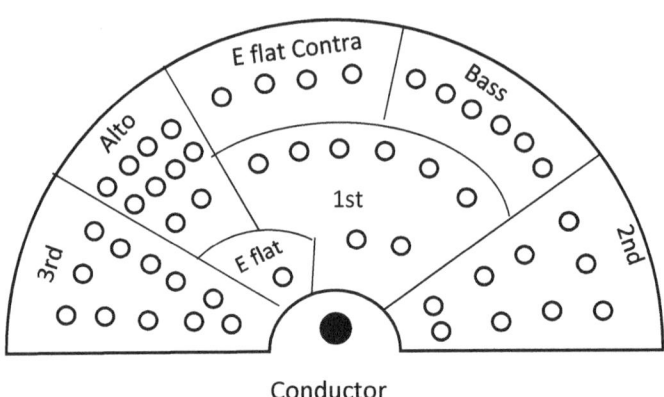

Conductor

To avoid difficulties in seating plans, the conductor should first pay the closest attention to the tonal balance of the choir. While an inadequate set-up can appreciably disrupt a performance, a carefully thought-out seating plan can ensure the performance becomes a satisfying musical experience for performers and listeners alike. While there is in fact no ideal lay-out, if you aim to achieve an ideal sound, this will always be crowned with success.

3 Contexts of historical genres

3.1 Does the clarinet choir constitute a genre?

As this section is consciously formulated as a question, it should be subject to clarification, so we first need to establish criteria for evaluating musical genres.

Many distinguished music theorists have already considered the question of musical genres and their social background. To date, the standardisa-tion of criteria for the classification of music into genres has only been partially successful.

In this context, Walter Wiora defines as starting points, 'leading ideas', the crystallising into models, but also longer lasting types [of ensemble][137] Wolfgang Suppan mentions in his article 'The Clarinet Duet' that early op-portunities to play together as a duo and their primary human use constitute a timely and spatially far-reaching 'leading idea' which in the world's differ-ent cultures have led to model specialisations.[138] Carl Dahlhaus talks of common features of the function, of a text or type of en-semble through which works are connected with each other. Dahlhaus continues, 'These criteria are a necessary, if not sufficient, precondition that there are enough combinations to constitute a genre, although they don't exist in isolation from each other either: Expressed briefly, the genres of an epoch form a system which is both hierarchical and also characterised by similarities and

---

[137] cf. Walter Wiora, 'Methodik der Musikwissenschaft', [Methodology of Musicology] in: Enzyklopädie der geisteswissenschaftlichen Arbeitsmethoden, München/Wien, 1970, p. 128.
[138] Wolfgang Suppan, 'Das Klarinetten-Duett', in: *Festschrift zum 65. Geburtstag von Ludwig Finscher*, Kassel inter alia, 1995, p. 289 ff.

contrasts'.[139] Hence Dahlhaus maintains the String Quintet does not constitute its own genre, because individual quintets refer not to each other,
but rather to their respective Quartet[s] by the same composer.[140]

The Clarinet Choir (comprising E flat Clarinet, 1st, 2nd & 3rd Clarinets,
Bass Clarinet and Contrabass Clarinet) fulfils some of the require-ments for
genres completely and there is no doubt that it possesses a 'leading idea' at
its core, but the fact is, it also fulfils a fundamental social function and, as
we have already heard, that we now have a commonly agreed scoring which
connects works with each other. Since its beginnings in the 1920s, we can
trace the clarinet choir's specific features related to the technical development, the sound and instrumental technique, and associated in its social
history with its development in high school and college bands and the
American concert orchestras. According to Dahlhaus,

> that works are connected with each other by common features, by their
> function, their text or type of ensemble is a necessary, if not sufficient,
> precondition that there are enough combinations to constitute a
> genre.[141]

---

[139] Carl Dahlhaus, 'Zur Problematik der musikalischen Gattungen im 19. Jahrhundert',
[On the issue of musical genres] in: *Gattungen der Musik in Einzeldarstellungen. Gedenkschrift Leo Schrade*, ed. Wulf Arlt inter alia, Bern/München, 1973, pp. 840-895, citation
p. 851

[140] ibid. p. 842; cf. Hermann Danuser, ‚Funktions- und Gattungswandel', [Tranformation
of functions and genres] in: *Die Musik des 20. Jahrhunderts* (Neues Handbuch der Musikwissenschaft), Vol. 7, ed. Carl Dahlhaus, Laaber, 1984, pp. 166-194.

[141] ibid. p. 842.

In the Instrumentalist in 1955, George Waln, one of the pioneers of the Clarinet Choir Movement, wrote the following about the function of a clarinet choir:

Aside from the effectiveness of the clarinet choir as a concert ensemble, it has genuine value as a training group for the individual players. The values of the small ensemble in developing tonal concept, careful listening, good intonation and phrasing are all present in the clarinet choir. It is an excellent training group for improving the concert band.[142]

In this connection Norman Heim also commented:

[...] first, strictly as a training group for the clarinet section of the band; and second, as a performing group, separate from the band, with it's own programs and repertoire. This author feels that the most meaningful approach would be a combination of both the training and performing philosophies: thus, the student receives the benefit of playing in a smaller chamber group, but at the same time the group serves as a teaching laboratory for the band clarinet section.[143]

Although the contrabass clarinet emerged for the first time in American [Wind] Orchestras in 1930,[144] it was only in the 1950s that the whole clarinet family was involved in the many Concert and school orchestras. This

---

[142] cf. George Waln, 'The Clarinet Choir, It's Functions and Values', in: *The Instrumentalist*, Nov. 1955, p. 30.

[143] cf. Norman Heim, The Clarinet Choir, Purpose and Literature, in: *Wood World Brass*, Apr. 1975, p. 8.

[144] The University of Illinois Band used the Contrabass Clarinet for the first time in 1930; cf. George D. Stirrat, loc.cit. pp. 44-46; cf. also Raoul F. Camus, loc.cit. pp. 4-8.

should consequently be considered as the 'golden era' for the Clarinet Choir Movement in America.

A golden era was soon to dawn for the clarinet choir, stimulated by music educators seeking to improve their clarinet sections.[145]

So from the very start, 'Clarinet Choir Performance' is linked with the appearance on stage of the whole clarinet family. While the original intention of the pioneers was to raise the standard of the American Concert Orchestra by means of ensemble playing, by creating its own repertoire from its beginnings in the 1920s,[146] the clarinet choir of the 1950s was able to step into the limelight particularly in colleges and universities in the USA as a 'stand alone' ensemble.

Initially, Clarinet Choirs' performances mostly consisted of arrangements, of important musical works of the 17th, 18th and 19th Centuries adapted for this purpose. With the creation of its own repertoire in the early 1950s (see Ch. 1) and the crystallisation of its own type of medium, we can begin to talk of the Clarinet Choir as a separate entity [a specific genre] from around 1950, although it was still mainly its teaching features and training functions that stood in the foreground. So perhaps it is not enough simply to 'repeat a name so that musical works can be combined into a genre one can write history about.'[147] Dahlhaus writes that an instrumental group may only fulfil the criterion of a genre if it (like the String Quartet or Trio Sonata) adopts a type of technical principle.[148]

---

[145] John Morgan, loc.cit. pp. 767-769.
[146] cf. also Ch. 1 'Early Clarinet Ensembles'
[147] Carl Dahlhaus, loc.cit. p. 840.
[148] ibid. p. 846.

As it is possible to identify a multiplicity of genres among compositions, it would appear to be difficult to generalise about their stylistic, compositional and technical features here. To consider the crystallisation of models is beside the point in this context. It is not so much about the history of the specific genre to which possible works may or may not belong, but the question 'how far can we talk about the Clarinet Choir itself as a genre?'

Walter Wiora's suggestion seems entirely plausible to me, namely to de-fine as 'types' those 'products of musical qualities' which appear to be 'more specific than genres, but more general than individual pieces of music.'[149] According to this definition, the clarinet choir would be at most a 'type' of the genre 'wind chamber music'. This open definition seems appropriate in so far as (as Wolfgang Suppan says) 'a multitude of genres and variant types exist in constant fluctuations and combinations.'[150]

---

[149] Walter Wiora, loc.cit. p.128.

[150] Wolfgang Suppan, ‚Das Klarinetten-Duett‘, in: *Festschrift zum 65. Geburtstag von Ludwig Finscher*, Kassel inter alia, 1995, pp. 289-297.

4 Conclusion

It was primarily pedagogical considerations that encouraged clarinet choirs to flourish at the start of the Clarinet Choir Movement in the 1950s particularly in the USA. This is also supported by the [previously quoted] statement of Raoul Camus.[151]

In the context of the functionality and development of the Clarinet Choir in the USA and Japan, Alfred Reed's explanations are illuminating:

> I would say that this type of performing organization exists largely in the educational area: schools, colleges and universities, much the same as in the U.S. But there are one or two professional organizations which play a few public concerts each year...[152]

> Smaller clarinet groups are an important part of the music education system both in Japan and the USA i.e. trios, quartets, quintets, etc., and the larger clarinet choirs like those mentioned above have been developing during the past 35 years in both countries, both in the schools and as amateur groups for private performance and enjoyment.[153]

So we can conclude that the Clarinet Choir Movement in the USA mainly exists in the education sector. In Europe, the first Clarinet Choir was founded in November 1970 in the UK. The Ionian Clarinet Choir was founded in Whetstone by Ray Upton Holder, Music Director of the London Borough of Barnet.[154] The first Clarinet Choirs to be established in the

---

[151] cf. Raoul F. Camus, loc.cit. p. 12.
[152] Alfred Reed, loc.cit.
[153] ibid.
[154] cf. Norman Heim, loc.cit. p. 6.

rest of Europe were in Belgium and Holland in the 1980s. In these countries the Clarinet Choir now has a firm place in the musical landscape.

If the Clarinet Choir is to succeed in future as a stand-alone concert ensemble, this will certainly depend not least on whether enough original works of quality are written by composers and promoted by publishers. But the Clarinet Choir's many tonal and scoring possibilities allow us to hope that in the future Clarinet Choirs will function not just as a training ensembles in the education sector, but will make a name for themselves as fully fledged ensembles in their own right.

5 Bibliography

Abramson, A. R., 'A better Use of the Clarinet Choir', in: Woodwind Anthology. A Compendium of Woodwind Articles from *The Instrumentalist* [or Ed.], Vol. 2, Northfield, Ill. 1986, pp. 748-749.

Abravanel, Cl., The Simeon Bellison Archives at the Jerusalem Rubin Academy of Music and Dance, A Catalogue, Jerusalem, 1993.

Adorno, Th. W., *Philosophie der neuen Musik*, Frankfurt, 1997.

Adorno, Th. W., ,Einleitung in die Musiksoziologie', in: *Gesammelte Schriften* 14, 2. Ed, Frankfurt/Main 1980.

Ayres, T. A., 'Arranging for the Clarinet Choir', in: Woodwind Anthology. A Compendium of Woodwind Articles from *The Instrumentalist* [o. Hg.], Vol. 2, Northfield, Ill. 1986, pp. 691-693.

Baines, A., *Woodwinds Instruments and Their History*, New York, 1991.

Benade, A. H., 'Woodwinds. The Evolutionary Path Since 1700', in: *The Galpin Society Journal*, No. 47, Mar 1994, pp. 63-110.

Berendt, J. E., Uhde J., *Prisma der gegenwärtigen Musik. Tendenzen und Probleme des zeitgenössischen Schaffens*, Hamburg, 1959.

Bodendorff, W., *Historie der geblasenen Musik*, Buchloe, 2002.

Bogart, Jr., D. Th., 'A History of the Clarinet as an Orchestral Instrument from Inception to full Acceptance into the Woodwind Choir', unpublished doctoral dissertation, Michigan State University, Ph.D., Michigan, 1968.

Brixel, E., *Klarinetten-Bibliographie* I, Wilhelmshaven, 1978.

Brymer, J., ‚Die Klarinette‘, in: *Yehudi Menuhins Musikführer* (Ed.), Frankfurt am Main, 1983

Caillet, L., *Clarinet Choir Literature*, Kenosha, Wisconsin, 1962.

Cailliet, L., *The Clarinet and Clarinet Choir*, Kenosha, Wisconsin, 1955.

Camus, R. F., ‘Art. Bands’, in: *The New Grove Dictionary of American Music*, Vol. 1, ed. H. W. Hitchcock & S. Sadie, London 1986, p. 127-137.

Camus, R. F., ‚Blasmusik an amerikanischen Schulen‘, in: *Clarino Bläsermusik*, 12. Jg., 11/2001, pp. 10-13.

Camus, R. F., ‘Some Nineteenth-Century Band Journals’, in: *Festschrift zum 60. Geburtstag von Wolfgang Suppan*, Tutzing 1993, p. 336.

Chatwin, R. B., ‘Händel and the Clarinet’, in: *The Galpin Society Journal*, No. 3, March 1950, pp. 3-8.

Cibulka, F., ‚Die Klarinette in Kammermusikwerken (Duo - Quintett) steirischer Komponisten des 20. Jahrhunderts‘, Magister Arbeit Musikhochschule Graz, 1994.

Cipolla, F. J., Hunsberger, D., (Ed.), *The Wind Ensemble and its Repertoire. Essays on the Fortieth Anniversary of the Eastman Wind Ensemble*, New York, 1994.

Closson, E., Richard Strauss. *Le Traité d'Orchestration d'Hector Berlioz* (Commentaire et Adjonctions Coordonnées et Traduits), Leipzig, 1909.

Cohen, A., ‘A Study of Instrumental Ensemble Practice in Seventeenth-Century France’, in: *The Galpin Society Journal*, No. 15, Mar 1962, pp. 3-17.

Cooper, M., *The Modern Age* (1890-1960), London, inter alia 1974.

Dahlhaus, C., ‚Zur Problematik der musikalischen Gattungen im 19. Jahrhundert', in: *Gattungen der Musik in Einzeldarstellungen. Gedenkschrift Leo Schrade*, ed. Wulf Arlt inter alia, Bern/München, 1973.

Dahlhaus, C., ‚Analyse und Werturteil', in: *Musikpädagogik. Forschung und Lehre*, Vol. 8, ed. Sigrid Abel-Struth, Mainz, 1970.

Dahlhaus, C., Mayer, G., ‚Musiksoziologische Reflexionen - Zur Theorie der musikalischen Gattungen', in: Dahlhaus, C., (Ed.), *Neues Handbuch der Musikwissenschaft*, Vol. 10, Wiesbaden, 1982.

Dahlhaus, C., Zimmermann, M., (Ed.), *Musik zur Sprache gebracht. Musikästhetische Texte aus drei Jahrhunderten*, München, 1984.

Danfelt, E. D., ‚The Clarinet Choir. A Means of Teaching and Performing Music', unpubl doctoral dissertation, University of Rochester, 1965.

Danuser, H., Motte-Habei, II., Leopold, S., Miller, N., (Ed), *Das musikalische Kunstwerk. Geschichte-Ästhetik-Theorie*, Festschrift zum 60. Geburtstag von Carl Dahlhaus, Laaber, 1988.

Danuser, H., (Hg.), *Gattungen der Musik und ihre Klassiker* (Publikationen der Hochschule für Musik und Theater Hannover, ed. Richard Jakoby), Vol. 1, Laaber 1988.

Danuser, H., *Die Musik des 20. Jahrhunderts*, (Neues Handbuch der Musikwissenschaft), Vol. 7, ed. Carl Dahlhaus, Laaber, 1984.

Danuser, H., Krummacher F., (Hg.), *Rezeptionsästhetik und Rezeptionsgeschichte in der Musikwissenschaft*, (Publikationen der Hochschule für Musik und Theater Hannover, ed. Richard Jakoby), Vol. 3, Laaber, 1991.

Dullat, G., *Klarinetten. Grundzüge ihrer Entwicklung*, Frankfurt, 2001.

Eberst, A., *Klarnet od A do Z*, Polskie, 1971.

Eliason, R. E., 'Oboe, Bassoons, and Bass Clarinets, made by Hartford Connecticut, Makers before 1815', in: *The Galpin Society Journal*, Nr. 30, May 1977, pp. 43-51.

Fink, M., Gstrein R., Mössmer, G., (Ed.), *Musica Privata. Die Rolle der Musik im privaten Leben*, Festschrift zum 65. Geburtstag von Walter Salmen, Innsbruck/Neu Rum, 1991.

Finscher, L., (Ed.), *Die Musik in Geschichte und Gegenwart*, Sachteil, Vol.5, Kassel, inter alia 1996ff.

Flotzinger, R., *Geschichte der Musik in Österreich*. Zum Lesen und Nachschlagen, Graz, inter alia 1988.

Flum, Robert A., Jr., 'The Use of the Alto, Bass, and Contrabass Clarinets in selected Wind Band Compositions written between 1951 and 1972', unpublished dissertation, University of Northern Colorado, Colorado, 1985.

Gibson, Lee O., *Clarinet Acoustics*, Bloomington, IN, 1998.

Gieseler, W., *Komposition im 20.Jahrhundert. Details - Zusammenhänge*, Celle, 1975.

Gillespie, Jr. J. E., *Solos for Unaccompanied Clarinet: An Annotated Bibliography of Published Works*, Detroit 1973.

Goldman, R. F., *The Wind Band. Its Literature and Technique* (Reprint of Edition from 1961), Westport, CT 1974.

Grass, Th., Demus D., *Das Bassetthorn. Seine Entwicklung und seine Musik*, 2. Ed., Norderstedt, 2004.

Harnoncourt, N., *Musik als Klangrede. Wege zu einem neuen Musikverständnis*, Salzburg und Wien, 1982.

Heim, N., ‚The Development of the Clarinet Choir in the USA‘, in: Bericht über die zweite internationale Fachtagung zur Erforschung der Blasmusik, Tutzing, 1977, pp. 109-120 *(Alta Musica 4)*.

Heim, N., 'The Clarinet Choir', in: Woodwind Anthology. A Compendium of Woodwind Articles from *The Instrumentalist* [o. Hg.], Vol. 2, Northfield, Ill. 1986, S. 1019-1020.

Heim, N., 'The Clarinet Choir Phenomenon', in: Woodwind Anthology. A Compendium of Woodwind Articles from *The Instrumentalist* [or Ed.], Vol. 2, Northfield, Ill. 1986, pp. 951-955.

Heim, N., (Ed.), 'Clarinet Choir'. *News International*, Vol 1-7, Hyattsville, Maryland, 1978-1982.

Heim, N., ‚William Schmidt. Master Wind Composer‘, Manuscript, Maryland 1995, p. 1.

Herrmann, Schneider-Hildegard, *Status und Funktion des Hofkapellmeisters in Wien* (1848-1918), Innsbruck/Neu Rum, 1981.

Hockett, V. J., 'The Role of the Clarinet as a Performance Ensemble with Emphasis on its Literature and History', M. A. Thesis, Northeast Missouri State College, 1972.

Hofer, A., *Blasmusikforschung. Eine kritische Einführung*, Darmstadt, 1992.

Hofer, A., ‚Gedanken zur Ästhetik von Blas- und Bläsermusik', in: Habla, B., (Ed.), *Festschrift zum 60. Geburtstag von Wolfgang Suppan*, Tutzing, 1993, pp. 265-273.

Hofer, A., ‚Harmoniemusik', in: *Die Musik in Geschichte und Gegenwart*, ed. von Ludwig Finscher, Sachteil Vol. 4, Kassel inter alia 1996, pp. 153-167.

Hofer, A., ‚Was ist Harmoniemusik? Annäherungen an eine Antwort', in: *Tibia* 20, 1995, pp. 577-585.

Höfer, M., ‚Frühe Sololiteratur für Bassklarinette - nebst einem kurzen Abriß der Entstehungsgeschichte des Instruments', in: *Rohrblatt*, Jg. 15, Vol. 4, pp. 166-170.

Holman, W. M., 'A Comprehensive Performance Project in Clarinet Literature with a History of the Society for the Publication of American Music 1919-1969', unpubl doctoral dissertation, University of Iowa, D.M.A. Thesis, Iowa, 1977.

Honegger M., Massenkeil, G., (Ed.), *Das große Lexikon der Musik*, Vols. 1-8, Freiburg inter alia, 1979.

Jesu, J. D., 'Improved Clarinet Section Via Choirs', in: Woodwind Anthology. A Compendium of Woodwind Articles from *The Instrumentalist* [or. Ed.], Vol.2, Northfield, Ill. 1986, pp. 665.

Jooste, St., ‚Der Beitrag der Militärmusik und der ‚zivilen' Blasmusik zur Kunstmusik Südafrikas im 19. Jahrhundert', in: W. Suppan und E. Brixel (Ed.), Kongreßbericht Mainz 1996, Tutzing, 1998, *(Alta Musica 20)*.

Jooste, St., ‚Der dt. Einfluß auf die abendl. Blasmusik Südafrikas von 1652 bis 1902', in: W. Suppan und E. Brixel (Ed.), Kongreßbericht Oberschützen 1988/Toblach, 1990, Tutzing, 1992, pp. 109-139 *(Alta Musica 14)*.

Jordan, D. M., *Alfred Reed. A Bio-Bibliography*, Westport, Connecticut & London, 1999.

Jost, M., *Die Bedeutung der Klarinette in der Kammermusik von Johannes Brahms*, Frechen, 2002.

Jungheinrich, H. K., *Unser Musikjahrhundert. Von Richard Strauss zu Wolfgang Rihm*, Salzburg, Wien, 1999.

Kalina, D. L., 'The Structural Development of the Bass Clarinet', unpubl doctoral dissertation, Columbia University, Ed. D., 1972.

Kalker, J. van., *Die Geschichte der Klarinetten*, Oberems 1997.

Klein, Lonnie, D., 'A comprehensive List of Literature for Clarinet Choir with Selected Analysis', unpubl doctoral dissertation, University of Illinois, Ph.D., Illinois 1993, pp. 21-22.

Knaus, H., Scholz, G., *Formen in der Musik. Herkunft, Analyse, Beschreibung*, Vol. 1, Wien, 1988.

Knaus, H., Scholz, G., *Formen in der Musik. Anregungen zur Musikanalyse*, Vol. 2, Wien, 1989.

Kolneder, W., ‚Die Klarinette als Concertino-Instrument bei Vivaldi', in: *Die Musikforschung* (Sonderdruck aus der Zeitschrift), Jg. 4, Vol 2/3, n.d.

Kroll, O., *Die Klarinette. Ihre Geschichte – Ihre Literatur – Ihre großen Meister*, ed. Diethard Riehm, (Reprint of 1965 Ed), Kassel inter alia, 1993.

Kunitz, H., *Die Instrumentation. Ein Hand - und Lehrbuch*, Leipzig, 1956.

Kühn, Cl., *Formenlehre der Musik*, 6th. Ed., Kassel inter alia, 2001.

Kühn, Cl., *Analyse lernen*, ed. Silke Leopold & Jutta Schmoll-Barthel, Vol. 4, 4th. Ed. Kassel inter alia, 2002.

Lawson, C., *The Cambridge Companion to the Clarinet*, Cambridge, United Kingdom, 1995.

Lawson, C., 'The Early Chalumeau Duets', in: *The Galpin Society Journal*, No. 27, May 1974, pp. 125-130.

Lawson, C., *The Early Clarinet. A practical Guide*, Cambridge, 2000.

Lawson, C., Stowell R., *The Historical Performance of Music: An Introduction*, Cambridge, 1999.

Lawson, C., *The Chalumeau in Eighteenth-Century Music*, Michigan, 1981.

Manfredo, J., 'Influences on the development of the Intrumentation of the American Collegiate Wind-Band and Attempts for Standardization of the Instrumentation from 1905-1941', in: W. Suppan & E. Brixel (Ed.), Tutzing, 1995 *(Alta Musica 17)*.

Marold, A., *Spiel in kleinen Gruppen*, Tutzing, 1999 (Alta Musica 21).

Mauser, S., (Ed.), *Handbuch der musikalischen Gattungen. Musiktheater im 20. Jahrhundert*, Vol. 14, Laaber, 2002.

Messenger J. Ch., 'A Comprehensive Performance Project in Clarinet Literature with an annotated Bibliography of selected Books and Periodical Material about the History, Repertoire, and Acoustics of the Clarinet', University of Iowa, Iowa, 1971.

Mitchell, J. C., 'The Kneller Hall Archives. The British Military Band Tradition in Manuscript', in: W. Suppan & E. Brixel (Ed.), Kongreßbericht Mainz, 1996, Tutzing, 1998 *(Alta Musica 20)*.

Morgan, J. B., 'The Clarinet Choir', M. M. Thesis, University of Michigan, 1962.

Morgan, J., 'The History of the Clarinet Choir', in: Woodwind Anthology. A Compendium of Woodwind Articles from *The Instrumentalist* [or. Ed], Vol. 2, Northfield, Ill. 1986, pp. 767-769.

Nowak, K. E., 'A Survey & Analysis of selected Clarinet Choir Literature for Use at the High School Level', A Thesis, Faculty of California State University, Fullerton, 1979.

Pfatschbacher, F., *Der Klarinettenchor*, Tutzing 2005.

Randall, D. M., 'A Comprehensive Performance Project in Clarinet Literature with an Essay on the Clarinet Duet from ca. 1715 to ca. 1825', unpubl doctoral dissertation, University of Iowa, D.M.A., Iowa, 1970.

Rau, U., ‚Die Kammermusik für Klarinette und Streichinstrumente im Zeitalter der Wiener Klassik‘, Phil. Diss., Saarbrücken, 1977.

Redfield, J., *Music. A Science and an Art*, New York, 1928.

Rehfeldt, Ph., *New Directions for Clarinet*, Berkeley & Los Angeles, CA, 1994.

Restle, C., Fricke H., (Ed.), *Faszination Klarinette*, München inter alia 2004.

Revelli, W. D., 'The Balanced Clarinet Choir', in: Woodwind Anthology. A Compendium of Woodwind Articles from *The Instrumentalist* [or Ed.], Vol. 2, Northfield, Ill. 1986, p. 667.

Rice, A. R., *The Baroque Clarinet*, Oxford 1992.

Rice, A. R., 'The Clarinet d'Amour & Basset Horn', in: *The Galpin Society Journal*, No. 39, Sept 1986, pp. 97-111.

Riehm, D., ,Die europäische Klarinette in der Kunstmusik', in: Ludwig Finscher (Ed.), *MGG*, Sachteil, Vol. 5, Kassel inter alia 1996, p. 177.

Riley, E., 'A Comprehensive performance project in Clarinet Literature with an Essay on the Quality Dimensions of Clarinet Tone: A Preliminary Investigation', University of Iowa, D.M.A., Iowa, 1977.

Ross, D. E., 'A Comprehensive Performance Project in Clarinet Literature with an organological Study of the Development of the Clarinet in the Eighteenth Century' (Volume I and II), unpubl doctoral dissertation, University of Iowa, Iowa, 1985.

Salmen, W., (Ed.), ,Der Sozialstatus des Berufsmusikers vom 17. bis 19. Jahrhundert.' Gesammelte Beiträge im Auftrag der *Gesellschaft für Musikforschung*, Kassel, 1971.

Sachs, C., *Real-Lexikon der Musikinstrumente*, New York, 1979.

Sadie, S., (Ed.), *The New Grove Dictionary of Music and Musicians*, Vols. 1-29, London – New York, 2001.

Sandner, W., ,Die Klarinette bei Carl Maria von Weber', in: Lothar Hoffmann-Erbrecht (Ed.), *Neue Musikgeschichtliche Forschungen*, Vol. 7, Wiesbaden, 1971.

Scholz. G., (Ed.), ‚Pluralismus analytischer Methoden.‘ Publikationen des *Instituts für Musikanalytik Wien*, Vol. 3, Frankfurt am Main, 1996.

Shackleton, N., 'Bass clarinet', in: *The New Grove Dictionary of Music and Musicians*, Vol. 2, London – New York 2001, pp. 862-864.

Shackleton, N., 'Basset-horn', in: ibid, pp. 867-869.

Shackleton, N., 'The Clarinet of Western art music', in: ibid, p. 902.

Shackleton, N., 'The Earliest Basset Horns', in: *The Galpin Society Journal*, No. 40, pp. 2-23.

Shaw, D. J., 'A Five-piece Wind Band in 1518', in: *The Galpin Society Jounal*, No. 43, Mar 1990, pp. 60-67.

Sirker, U., ‚Die Entwicklung des Bläserquintetts in der ersten Hälfte des 19. Jahrhunderts‘, in: *Kölner Beiträge zur Musikforschung*, ed. K. G. Fellerer, Vol. L, Regensburg, 1968.

Slonimsky N., Kuhn L., (Ed.), *Baker´s Biographical Dictionary of Musicians*, New York 2001.

Stephan, R., (Ed.), ‚Neue Wege der musikalischen Analyse‘, in: Veröffentlichungen des *Instituts für neue Musik und Musikerziehung Darmstadt*, Vol. 6, Berlin, 1967.

Stirrat, G. D., 'The Development and Use of the Clarinet Choir in the American Concert Band', unpubl Ed. D. dissertation, Columbia University, New York, 1968.

Stoneham M., Gillespie J. A, Clark D. L., *Wind Ensemble Sourcebook and Biographical Guide*, Westport, CT, 1997.

Stubbins, H. W., *The Art of Clarinetistry*, Michigan, 1974.

Stuckenschmidt, H. H., *Neue Musik*, Frankfurt/Main, 1981.

Suppan, A., ‚Blasmusik-Dissertationen in den USA', in: *Studia musicologica Academiae Scientiarum Hungaricae* 36, Budapest 1995, pp. 181-226.

Suppan, W. & Suppan, A., *Das Neue Lexikon des Blasmusikwesens*, 4th Ed., Freiburg-Tiengen, 1994.

Suppan, W., ‚Das Klarinetten Duett', in: *Festschrift zum 65. Geburtstag von Ludwig Finscher*, Kassel inter alia 1995, pp. 289-297.

Suppan, W., *Blasmusikforschung seit 1966. Eine Bibliographie*, ed. B. Habla, Tutzing, 2003.

Suppan, W., ‚Der musizierende Mensch. Eine Anthropologie der Musik', in: Abel-Struth, S. (Ed.), *Musikpädagogik* 10, Mainz, 1984.

Suppan W., ‚Die Harmoniemusik', in: *Festschrift zum 65. Geburtstag von Walter Salmen*, ed. M. Fink inter alia, Innsbruck 1991, pp. 151-165.

Suppan, W., *Werk und Wirkung. Musikwissenschaft als Menschen- und Kulturgüterforschung* (Musikethnologische Sammelbände), ed. von W. Suppan, Vol. 15-17, Tutzing, 2000.

Waln, G. E., 'The Clarinet Choir', in: Woodwind Anthology. A Compendium of Woodwind Articles from *The Instrumentalist* [o. Ed.], Vol. 2, Northfield, Ill. 1986, pp. 683-684.

Walther, J. G., *Musicalisches Lexicon oder Musicalische Bibliothec* (Studienausgabe im Neusatz des Textes und der Noten), ed. Friederike Ramm, Kassel inter alia, 2001.

Weerts, R. K., 'The Clarinet Choir as a Functional Ensemble', in: Woodwind Anthology. A Compendium of Woodwind Articles from *The Instrumentalist* [or. Ed.], Vol. 2, Northfield, Ill. 1986, pp. 800-803.

Weerts, R. K., 'Clarinet Choir Music', in: Woodwind Anthology. A Compendium of Woodwind Articles from *The Instrumentalist* [or. Ed.], Vol. 2, Northfield, Ill. 1986, pp. 747-748.

Weerts, R. K., 'The Clarinet Choir of Yesterday and Today', in: Woodwind Anthology. A Compendium of Woodwind Articles from *The Instrumentalist* [or.Ed.], Vol. 2, Northfield, Ill. 1986, p. 833.

Weiner, L. B., 'The Unaccompanied Clarinet Duet from 1825 to the Present: An Annotated Catalogue', phil. Diss. New York University 1980 (Rez. von Norman Heim), in: *Council for Research in Music Education* 71, Summer 1982, p. 63ff.

West, Ch. W., 'A Comprehensive Performance Project in Clarinet Literature with an Essay on Music for Woodwinds and Strings, Five to Thirteen Players, Composed between ca. 1900 and ca. 1973', unpubl doctoral dissertation, D.M.A., University of Iowa, Iowa, 1975.

Weston, P., *More Clarinet Virtuosi of the past*, London 1992.

Weston, P., *Clarinet Virtuosi of the past*, London, 1994.

Whitwell, D., *Band Music of the French Revolution*, ed. W. Suppan & E. Brixel, Tutzing, 1979 (*Alta Musica* Vol. 5).

Whitwell, D., *The History of the Band and Wind Ensemble*, Vol. 1-9, Northridge, CA, 1982-1984.

Wilkins, W., *The Index of Clarinet Music*, Magnolia, Arkansas, 1975.

6 Repertoire Lists

As there is such an immense amount of material, this Repertoire List for Clarinet Choir does not set out to be anything like exhaustive and should only to be seen as a small catalogue.

Alongside arrangements this collection includes very many original works which can certainly be considered as standard repertoire.

It is also worth mentioning that Social Media and Networks shouldn't be ignored in looking for new material.

A real treasure trove of good arrangements is the *Hermann Clarinet Choir Music Collection*[155] by Illinois Clarinet Choir Pioneer Harvey Hermann.

The *ICA Score Collection*[156] at the University of Maryland also deserves a special mention, not least as repository of lots of original works. These days on the Internet it is relatively easy to research suitable up to date literature online at the relevant publishers and libraries.

---

[155] cf. www.dfapam.com/clarinetchoir/2006pricelist.pdf [accessed 24.07.2017]
[156] cf. www.lib.umd.edu/scpa/ [accessed 24.07.2017]; see also Friedrich Pfatschbacher, *Der Klarinettenchor*, Tutzing, 2005.

6.1 Combined Repertoire List

The following Repertoire List is arranged according to the following structure:

1. Composer's surname, 2. First name, 3. Title of the composition (also arranger), 4. Publisher (if available)

Surname	First	Title	Publisher
Aegler	Gottfried	Schweizer Volksmusik	Aegler
Albinoni	Tomaso	Concerto "Saint Marc" (arr. W. Schmidt)	Western
Alexander	William	Fantasy on plainchants from Salisbury	AMC
Alla	Thierry	Lunaire (14 Klar.)	Fuzeau
Almila	Atso	A Mario	FIMIC
Amos	Keith	Mr. Fothergill´s Sunday	CMA
Anderson	Leroy	Blue Tango (arr. C. Custer)	Maecenas
Anderson	Leroy	The Waltzing Cat (arr. R. van der Wal)	Maecenas
Anonyme		Grandfather's Clock (arr. M. Brand)	Vandoren
Anonyme		Sounds & Rounds (arr. M. Brand)	Vandoren
Appledorn	Mary J. van	Ayre	Southern
Arma	Paul	Douze Instantanés	Billaudot
Bach	J. Christian	Allegro aus Sinfonie Nr. 2 (arr. Voxman)	Rubank
Bach	J. Sebastian.	Brandenburg Concerto No. 1	Hilltop
Bach	J. Sebastian	Brandenburg Concerto No. 2	Hilltop
Bach	J. Sebastian	4 Choräle (arr. Johnston)	Shawnee
Bach	J. Sebastian	Air aus Orchestersuite Nr. 3 (arr. Sacci)	Kendor
Bach	J. Sebastian	Alla breve (arr. R. Dishinger)	Medici
Bach	J. Sebastian	Allein Gott in der Höh (arr. Dishinger)	Medici
Bach	J. Sebastian	Bach Suite (arr. P. Yoder)	Southern
Bach	J. Sebastian	Canzona (arr. R. Dishinger)	Medici
Bach	J. Sebastian	Celebrated Air (arr. Cl. W. Johnson)	Halter
Bach	J. Sebastian	Chorale "Sleepers awake" (arr. L. Caillet)	Southern

Bach	J. Sebastian	Christmas Oratorio (arr. R. Hervig)	Rubank
Bach	J. Sebastian	Fuge (arr. R. Dishinger)	Medici
Bach	J. Sebastian	Fuge (arr. E. Curry)	
Bach	J. Sebastian	Fuge Nr. 10 (arr. R. Dishinger)	Medici
Bach	J. Sebastian	„Little"- Fugue in G minor (1994)	Hakari
Bach	J. Sebastian	O Mensch, Bewein (arr. P. Grainger)	RSM
Bach	J. Sebastian	Präludium und Fuge D Minor (arr. Hite)	Southern
Bach	J. Sebastian	Preludes, Allemande und Courantes aus den 4 Sonaten (arr. Corroyez)	Billaudot
Bach	J. Sebastian	Puer Natus in Bethlehem (arr. R. Hervig)	Rubank
Bach	J. Sebastian	Trio d-Moll (arr. R. Dishinger)	Medici
Bach	Friedemann	Grave (arr. R. Dishinger)	Medici
Bailey	Anthony	College Counterpoint	Trio
Bailey	Anthony	Towards the Wind	Trio
Ball	Michael	Concertino	Studio Music
Balsac	Jean Claude	Bénit soit-il	
Barat	J. Ed.	Piece en Sol mineur (arr. G. F. Roach)	Southern
Barber	Samuel	Adagio for Strings (arr. L. Cailliet)	Schirmer
Barker	Warren	Sketches from America	
Baron	Maurice	The Last Tryst	Southern
Bartók	Béla	Folksong Suite (arr. F. Erickson)	Schirmer
Bartok	Béla	Roumanian Folk Dances (S. Kabayashi)	Bravo
Becheri	Roberto	Dissolvenze Incrociate (7 Klar.)	Pizzicato
Beethoven	Ludwig van	Adagio aus Klaviersonate "Pathetique" (arr. Cl. W. Johnson)	Rubank
Beethoven	Ludwig van	Für Elise (arr. L. Conley)	Kendor
Beethoven	Ludwig van	Ode to Joy	Kendor
Beethoven	Ludwig van	Rondino	Hilltop
Beethoven	Ludwig van	Scherzo uit octet, Op. 13 (arr. Johnson)	Rubank
Benoit	Peter	Fantasia 3, op. 18 (arr. J. De Doncker)	de haske
Benoit	Peter	Luim (arr. Joh. De Doncker)	de haske
Berlin	Irvin	Puttin on the Ritz (arr. A. Frankenpohl)	Kendor
Bernstein	Leonard	West Side Story (arr. Rutherford)	
Bizet	Georges	Adagietto aus "L'Arlésienne" (arr. Cailliet)	Southern

Bizet	Georges	Gypsy Dance aus "Carmen" (arr. Conley)	Kendor
Bloch	Ernest	Prelude and Processional (arr. J. O'Reilly)	Schirmer
Blyton	Carey	Fanfare and Royal March Op. 77	Reynard
Bois	Rob du	Fleeting (1977)	Donemus
Bois	Rob du	Iguanadon	Donemus
Boon	Michael	Gypsy Baron Overture	Cimarron
Borgo	Elliot del	Dodecaphonic Essay (1978)	Kendor
Borgo	Elliot del	Dona nobis pacem (arr.)	Kendor
Borgo	Elliot del	Irish Suite (arr.)	Kendor
Borodin	Alexander	Nocturne (arr. S. Nestico)	Kendor
Boyce	William	Sinfonie Nr. 4, 1. Satz (arr. del Borgo)	Kendor
Bozza	Eugene	Lucioles pour Ensemble de Clarinettes	Leduc
Brahms	Johannes	Chorale Prelude Nr. 8 (arr. R. Fote)	Kendor
Brahms	Johannes	Motette op. 29, Nr. 1 (H. Voxman)	Rubank
Brahms	Johannes	Cradle Song (arr. L. Lucchetta)	Kendor
Brahms	Johannes	Hungarian Dance (arr. F. Halferty)	Kendor
Brahms	Johannes	String Quintet Nr. 1 (arr. Mac Leod)	MacLeod
Bratton	John	The Teddy Bears Picnic (arr. Riss-Jensen)	R.-Jensen
Bullard	Alan	Circular Melody	Harlequin
Bullard	Alan	Cyclic Harmony	Harlequin
Butterworth	Arthur	Ludwigstanz Op. 56 (1975)	Comus
Buxtehude	Dietrich	Fugue (arr. R. Brown)	WIM
Buxtehude	Dietrich	Praeludium (arr. N. Heim)	WIM
Buxtehude	Dietrich	Toccate e fuga (arr. L. J. Coeck) (1991)	Southern
Cacavas	John	Two Miniatures	Southern
Cailliet	Lucien	Canzonetta 2	Leblanc
Cailliet	Lucien	Caprice Sentimental for Solo Cl. (1958)	Leblanc
Cailliet	Lucien	Carnival (1963)	Southern
Caillet	Lucien	Fantasie	Southern
Cailliet	Lucien	Clarinet Poem	Southern
Cannon	Hughie	Bill Bailey (arr. J. Christensen)	Kendor
Cardon	Roland	3 Shortys	Ande
Cardon	Roland	Prelude	Ande
Carrera	Pedro	Versets (arr. R. Brown)	WIM

Cartney	Paul Mc.	Yesterday (Y. Gourhand)	IMD
Carvalho		L`Amore Industrioso (arr. Wyver)	Hilltop
Casteel	D.	Londonderry Air	Kendor
Celis	Frits	Incantations	
Chiarparin	Antonio	Omaggio a Zoltan Kodaly	Pizzicato
Christensen	James	When the Saints Go Marching In (arr.)	Kendor
Cibulka	Franz	Clariphonic	Cibulka
Clarke	Frederick R.	Suite	CMC
Clarke	Frederick R.	Trumpet Voluntary (arr. R. Dishinger)	Medici
Clérisse	Robert	Vieille Chanson (arr. G. Roach)	Southern
Cohn	James	Caprice	
Coleridge	Samuel	Waltzes	Hilltop
Cooke	Arnold	Septet for Clarinets	World
Corelli	Arcangelo	Folie d´ Espagne (arr. A. Morris)	Pro Art
Corelli	Arcangelo	Kirchensonate (arr. J. Thornton)	Southern
Corette	Michel	Concerto Comique (Cl. Crousier)	Fuzeau
Couperin	Francoise	The Sailor's Song (arr. R. Dishinger)	Medici
Cowles	Colin	Paen	Studio
Crawley	Clifford	Harlequinade	CMC
Crousier	Claude	Tourbillons	Fuzeau
Cunnigham	Michael G.	Coloratura Op. 80 (1978)	Dorn
Debussy	Claude	Le Petit Negre (arr. A. Bailey)	Nieuwe
Debussy	Claude	Nuages (L. Conley)	Kendor
Debussy	Cluade	Petite Suite (arr. R. Howland)	Fema
Debussy	Claude	Sarabande (arr. S. Davis)	WIM
Desportes	Yvonne	Charactères	Billaudot
Dodgson	Stephen	Epigrams from A Garden (1977)	BMIC
Dondeyne	Désiré	Marche promenade (1994)	Billaudot
Dondeyne	Désiré	Symphonie des Clarinettes	Billaudot
Donizetti	Gaetano	Don Pasquale Overture (L. Anderson)	Jeanne
Dvorák	Antonin	Menuett aus der Serenade op. 44 C. W. Johnson)	(arr.Rubank
Dvorák	Antonin	String Quintet (arr. Ellis-MacLeod)	MacLeod
Eerola	Lasse	Scenes from Northern Carelia	FIMIC

Ellerby	Martin	Looping the Loop	
Fagerudd	Markus	The Carousell	FIMIC
Fauré	Gabriel	Pavane (arr. D. Farnon)	G&M Brand
Fisher	Aidan	Refrain (1995)	
Foster	Stephen	Jeanie with the Light Brown Hair (arr.)	De Stefano
Foster	Stephen	Stephen Foster Jazz Suite	Kendor
Frackenohl	Arthur	Ballad for George	Shawnee
Frackenpohl	Arthur	Licorice Licks	Kendor
Frackenpohl	Arthur	Prelude and Allegro (1969)	Shawnee
Franck	Cesar	Panis angelicus (arr. J. de Jesu)	Chas. Colin
Frescobaldi	Girolamo	Ricercare (arr. J. Underwood)	Kendor
Fucik	Julius	Einzug der Gladiatoren (arr. Goddard)	Spartan
Gabriele	Giovanni	Canzona per Sonare No. 2 (arr. Ayres)	Barnhouse
Garland	Joe	In the mood (C. Custer)	Belwin
Gates	Everet	Seasonal Sketches	Southern
Geoffrey	Coleby	Rags for Brass Quintett	Boosey
Gerber	Renae	A Terpsichore	Pizzicato
Gershwin	George	Fascinating Rhythm (arr. J. Power)	Power music
Gershwin	George	Prelude Nr. 2	Nleuwe
Gluck	Christoph W.	Hymnus aus "Iphigenie in Tauris" (arr. Th. T. Donley)	Medici
Goddaer	Norbert	Paganinesque	Lantro
Goddaer	Norbert	Theme and Dance	Lantro
Gordon	Jacob	Introduction and Rondo	Boosey
Gordon	Philip	Capriccio	Kendor
Gottschalk		Caprice (arr. R. Dishinger)	Medici
Grainger	Percy A.	Molly on the Shore (arr. St. Knight)	Cimarron
Grainger	Percy A.	Australian Up Contry Tune (arr. Allen)	
Grainger	Percy A.	Walking Tune (S. D. Farquhar)	Splunge
Graupner	Christoph	Sonata in G	Schirmer
Grieg	Edward	An der Wiege Op. 68 (arr. H. Voxman)	Rubank
Grieg	Edward	Holberg Suite (arr. R. Denwood) (2000)	Kendor
Grieg	Edward	In der Halle des Bergkönigs (arr. Hine)	Harlequin
Grieg	Edward	Lyrisches Stück Nr. 2 (arr. H. Voxman)	Rubank

Grieg	Edward	Norwegischer Tanz (arr. T. Fino)	Kendor
Grieg	Edward	Norwegischer Tanz Nr. 1-4 (arr. R. Denwood)	Kendor
Groot	B. de	Het land van Maas en Waal (arr. Maintz)	
Grundman	Clare	Caprice for Clarinets	Boosey
Händel	Georg F.	Air & Gigue from 12 Concerti Grossi (arr. H. Voxman)	Rubank
Händel	Georg F.	Chaconne (arr. E. Del Borgo)	Kendor
Händel	Georg F.	Concerto in F Minor	Shawnee
Händel	Georg F.	Julius Caesar Ouvertüre(arr. D. Wilcox)	Shawnee
Händel	Georg F.	Konzert (arr. Anderson)	Shawnee
Händel	Georg F.	Larghetto (arr. F. Sacci)	Kendor
Händel	Georg F.	Largo und Allegretto (arr. D. Hite)	Southern
Händel	Georg F.	Largo aus „Xerxes" (arr. Findlay)	Fischer
Händel	Georg F.	Marsch aus „Joshua" (arr. Th. T. Donley)	Medici
Händel	Georg F.	Messias Ouvertüre (arr. K. E. Webb)	Kendor
Händel	Georg F.	Pastoral Symphony (arr. K. E. Webb)	Kendor
Händel	Georg F.	Sarabande (arr. R. Dishinger)	Medici
Händel	Georg F.	Sarabande und Bourree (arr. K. Webb)	Kendor
Händel	Georg F.	Sarabande und Allegro aus dem Concerto Grosso Nr. 3 (arr. Voxman)	Rubank
Händel	Georg F.	Sonate Nr. 5 (arr. R. Dishinger)	Medici
Handy	William C.	St. Louis Blues (arr. J. Christensen)	Kendor
Hanna	W. & B.	The Flintstones (arr. J. van der Goot)	Muzika
Harris	Paul	Clarinetwise (2001)	Queen's
Hart	Paul	Eric's Czardas (1996)	Harlequin
Harvey	Paul	Dances of Atlantis (1997)	Harlequin
Harvey	Paul	El Torneo	Reynard
Harvey	Paul	Happijazz	Harlequin
Harvey	Paul	Jollipop	Harlequin
Harvey	Paul	Rockabelly	Harlequin
Harvey	Paul	The Keel Rock	Harlequin
Harvey	Paul	Sinfonietta	Harlequin
Haydn	Josef	Divertimento Nr. 1 (arr. R. Hindsley)	Southern

Haydn	Josef	Feld-Parthie in C (arr. P. Wastall)	Boosey
Haydn	Josef	Feld Parthie in F (arr. P. Wastall)	Boosey
Haydn	Josef	Presto aus dem Quartett Nr. 17, Op. 3	Pro Art
Haydn	Josef	Sinfonie Nr. 100. Daraus: 2. Satz (arr. Cl. W. Johnson)	Rubank
Haydn	Josef	Symphonie Nr. 85 – La Reine	Hilltop
Haydn	Josef	Sinfonie Nr. 88. Daraus: Menuett und Trio (arr. H. Feldsher)	Kendor
Heim	Norman	Symphonic Sketches	Norcat
Hennagin	Michael	4 Etudes	
Hidas	Frigyes	Three Sketches for Clarinet Choir (1988)	EMB
Hite	David L.	Vienna Baroque Suite (arr. Cl. W. Johnson)	Ludwig
Holt	Darrell	Blues for Stephanie	
Horner	James	My heart will go on (arr. L. Moore)	Leonard
Hughes	Eric	Celebration Overture	Harlequin
Hummel	Johann N.	Marche Romaine (arr. Wyver)	Hilltop
Hummel	Johann N.	Rondo from Concerto for Trumpet (arr. W. Schmidt)	WIM
Hurum	Helge	Kropps-Holdninger (1975)	NMIC
Hurum	Helge	Mosaic: Suite for Clarinet Choir (arr. W. Schmidt)	Norsk
Hurum	Helge	Mosaik (1983)	NMIC
Hutchinson	Warner	Suite for Clarinet Choir	Kendor
Hyman	Dick	Sextet for Clarinets	Kendor
Ingalls	Matt	Naked Time (1992)	M. Ingalls
Jacob	Gordon	Introduction and Rondo (1973)	Boosey
Jacob	Gordon	Wind in the Reeds (1983)	Studio
Janacek	Leos	Allegretto aus der 1. Sinfonietta	N. Lent
Johnson	Clair W.	Scherzo capriccio	Rubank
Kander	John	Theme from New York (C. Custer)	Belwin
Karel	Leon	Elegy and Dance (arr. L. Caillet) (1965)	Southern
Joplin	Scott	The Chrysanthemum (arr. W. Schmidt)	WIM

Karg-Elert	Siegfried	Now thank we all our God (arr. Heim)	Kendor
Khachaturian	Aram	Armenian Song (arr. A. Estes)	Kendor
Kirkwood	Derick	A Robert Burns Fantasy	Iatona
Kirkwood	Derick	Ayrshire Clarinets	Iatona
Klauss	Noah	Dolce (with a beat)	Kendor
Klauss	Noah	Clarinetics	Emerson
Klauss	Noah	Electronic Brain	Kendor
Knight	Steve	Mock Morris	Cimarron
Koepke	Paul	Allegro Rococo	Rubank
Krell	W. H.	Mississippi Rag (arr. Frackenpohl)	Kendor
Krenek	Ernst	Three Short Pieces, Op. 83 (arr. F. Erickson) (1969)	Schirmer
Kreutzer	Konradin	Prayer (arr. Th. T. Donley)	Medici
Kubizek	Wolfgang	Fickle Decissions	
Kupferman	Meyer	A Little Licorice Concerto	Dorn
Küffner	Josef	Introduktion, Thema und Variationen (arr. P. Harvey)	Harlequin
Lasso	Orlando di	Echo Song (arr. R. Hall)	Eight Note
Legrenzi	Giovanni	La Buscha. Sonata (arr. Chr. Vadala)	Medici
Lennon	& McCartney	When I'm Sixty Four (arr. P. Riss-Jensen)	R.-Jensen
Lerstad	Terje B.	Adagio for Contrabass, Op. 113 D (1986)	NMIC
Lerstad	Terje B.	Elise Onder de Oliphant, Op. 151 (1982)	NMIC
Lerstad	Terje B.	Gloria, Op. 115 (1977/80)	NMIC
Lerstad	Terje B.	Incantations, Op. 103 B (1977)	NMIC
Lerstad	Terje B.	Madamme de la Mountaine…, Op. 11	NMIC
Lerstad	Terje B.	Mirrors in Ebony, Op. 114 (1981)	NMIC
Lerstad	Terje B.	Ouverture for Clarinet Choir (1974)	NMIC
Lerstad	Terje B.	Allegro for 16 Clarinets, Op. 10 (1969)	NMIC
Lerstad	Terje B.	Suite for Clarinet Choir, Op. 103 A	NMIC
Lewin	Gordon	Calle de Flores	Harlequin
Lewin	Gordon	The Grand Old Duke of York (1995)	Harlequin
Lewin	Gordon	Grass Roots	Harlequin
Lewin	Gordon	Hava nagila (arr.)	Brasswind

Linkola	Jukka	Chalumeaux-Suite	FIMIC
Logothetis	Anestis	Emanation	
Loucheur	Raymond	En famille (1970)	Billaudot
Livingston	J. & Evans	Silver Bells (arr. C. Calvin)	Belwin
Lumbye	H. C.	Champagne Galop (arr. M. Wehding)	Wemus
Lunde	Ivar jr.	Nuances, Op. 55 (1975)	Kendor
MacDowell	Edward A.	Woodland Sketches (arr. N. Heim)	Kendor
Mancini	Henry	Charade (arr. J. Fairhead)	Cascade
Mancini	Henry	The Pink Panther (arr. C. Custer)	Belwin
Marcello	Benedetto	Psalm eighteen (arr. N. Heim)	Kendor
Martin	Hugh & Bl.	Have yourself a merry little christmas (arr. C. Custer)	Maecenas
Massenet	Jules	Angelus (arr. L. Cailliet)	Southern
Masser	Michael	The greatest love of all (arr. C. Custer)	Belwin
McCathren	Don	Electronic Brain (arr. N. Klauss)	Kendor
Mendelssohn	Felix	Allegro Vivace 5. Symph. (arr. H. Feldsher)	Pro Art
Mendelssohn	Felix	Dance of the clowns (arr. Th. T. Donley)	Medici
Mendelssohn	Felix	Fingal's Cave Overture (arr. D. Freeman)	
Mendelssohn	Felix	Saltarello aus der 4. Symph. (Howland)	Wingert
Mendelssohn	Felix	Tarantella, Op. 102, Nr. 3 (arr. K. Webb)	Kendor
Menken	Alan	Aladdin (arr. J. van der Goot)	Muzika
Mestrom	Maarten	Sinfonietta for Clarinet Choir	Trio
Miller	Glennn	Moonlight serenade (arr. C. Custer)	Belwin
Molter	J. Melchior	Konzert Nr. 3 (arr. L. Anderson)	Jeanne
Morales	E.	Two Spanish Renaissance Works (arr. R. Dishinger)	Medici
Mozart	Wolfgang A.	Adagio (arr. H. Voxman)	Rubank
Mozart	Wolfgang A.	Adagio from Quintett in G Minor (arr. F. Sacci)	Kendor
Mozart	Wolfgang A.	Adagio aus der Serenade Nr. 11 in Eb (arr. P. Wastall)	Boosey
Mozart	Wolfgang A.	Allegro maestoso (arr. F. Sacci)	Kendor
Mozart	Wolfgang A.	Allegro and Allegretto from Div. Nr. 2 (arr. L. Danfelt) (1974)	Shawnee

Mozart	Wolfgang A.	Andante aus dem Divertimento (Thilde)	Kendor
Mozart	Wolfgang A.	Andante und Rondo aus dem Horn Konzert (arr. F. Sacci)	Kendor
Mozart	Wolfgang A.	Andante aus Divertimento Nr. 1 (arr. M. Reid)	Kendor
Mozart	Wolfgang A.	Ave Verum Corpus (arr. Th. T. Donley)	Medici
Mozart	Wolfgang A.	Chorus from the Magic Flute (arr. Th. T. Donley)	Medici
Mozart	Wolfgang A.	Contredanse (arr. Y. Bouchet)	IMD
Mozart	Wolfgang A.	Cosi Fan Tutte. Overture (arr. D. Casteel & McCathren)	Kendor
Mozart	Wolfgang A.	Die Hochzeit des Figaros (arr. L. Caillet)	Southern
Mozart	Wolfgang A.	Divertimento Nr. 6 (arr. Cl. W. Johnson)	Rubank
Mozart	Wolfgang A.	Eine kleine Nachtmusik (arr. J. Lancelot)	Billaudot
Mozart	Wolfgang A.	Eine kleine Nachtmusik (arr. Trebsche)	Reimers
Mozart	Wolfgang A.	Eine kleine Nachtmusik. Daraus: 1. Satz (arr. F. Sacci)	Kendor
Mozart	Wolfgang A.	Eine kleine Nachtmusik. Daraus: 2. Satz (arr. F. Sacci)	Kendor
Mozart	Wolfgang A.	Eine kleine Nachtmusik. Daraus: 3. Satz (arr. Cl. Johnson)	Rubank
Mozart	Wolfgang A.	Eine kleine Nachtmusik. Daraus: 3. Satz (arr. F. Sacci)	Kendor
Mozart	Wolfgang A.	Eine kleine Nachtmusik. Daraus: 4. Satz (arr. F. Sacci)	Kendor
Mozart	Wolfgang A.	aus der Symph. Nr. 36 (arr. van der Wal)	Rubank
Mozart	Wolfgang A.	Polonaise und Presto aus dem Div. Nr. 12 (arr. R. Hervig)	
Mozart	Wolfgang A.	Quadrille (arr. Y. Bouchet)	IMD
Mozart	Wolfgang A.	Quintett (arr. Ellis-MacLeod)	MacLeod
Mozart	Wolfgang A.	Rondo Alla Turca (arr. A. Bailey)	Harlequin
Mozart	Wolfgang A.	Rondo from Serenade No. 10 (arr. Pillin)	WIM
Mozart	Wolfgang A.	The Marriage of Figaro (arr. Howland)	Fema
Mozart	Wolfgang A.	Serenade Nr. 1, Menuetto (arr. H. Voxman)	Rubank

Mozart	Wolfgang A.	Sinfonia Concertante KV 279 b (arr. M. Frankton)	Music for Winds
Mozart	Wolfgang A.	Sinfonietta in B (arr. F. Frackenpohl)	Shawnee
Mozart	Wolfgang	Türkischer Marsch (arr. K. Morita)	Bravo
Nelhýbel	Václav	Chorale and Danza	Southern
Nelhybel	Václav	Peter Piber	Southern
Nelhybel	Vaclav	Ricercare for Clar. and Sax. Choir (1966)	Southern
Nestico	Sammy	A Study in Contrast	Kendor
Niehaus	Lennie	A Christmas Jazz Portrait	Kendor
Niehaus	Lennie	All Too Soon	Kendor
Niehaus	Lennie	Christmas Jazz Favorites (arr.) 3 Bände	Kendor
Niehaus	Lennie	Clarinetwork	Kendor
Niehaus	Lennie	Gay 90's Jazz Suite (1993)	Kendor
Niehaus	Lennie	Jubilation	Kendor
Niehaus	Lennie	Miniature Jazz Suite Nr. 1	Kendor
Niehaus	Lennie	Popular American Songs. 2 Bände	Kendor
Niehaus	Lennie	Spiritual Jazz Suite	Kendor
Niehaus	Lennie	Stephen Foster Jazz Suite	Kendor
Niehaus	Lennie	Wood Tacks	Kendor
Niehaus	Lennie	Yuletide Jazz Suite. 2 Bände	Kendor
Ostransky	Leroy	Andante und Rondo	Rubank
Owen	Harold	Fantasies on Mexican Tunes (1981)	WIM
Pachelbel	Johann	Kanon (arr. A. Suppan)	Kliment
Pagotto	Mario	Anche i sogni danzano?	Pizzicato
Paradis	Maria T. von	Sicilienne (arr. A. Blank)	Roncorp
Parfrey	Raymond	A March of Moods	Comus
Payne	Frank Lynn	Miniaturen	Seesaw
Pezel	Johann Chr.	Three Pieces	Kendor
Pezel	Johann Chr.	Sonate Nr. 38 (arr. R. Dishinger)	Medici
Pezel	Johann Chr.	Sonate Nr. 4 (arr. R. Dishinger)	Medici
Presser	M.	Choral Fantasy (1962)	Southern
Prokofiev	Serge	Peter und der Wolf (arr. J. van der Goot)	Muzika
Pugnani	Gaetano	Menuetto (arr. R. Dishinger)	Medici
Purcell	Henry	Sonata (arr. D. Marlatt)	Eight Note

Rachmaninof	Sergei	Moment Musical Nr. 3 (arr. W. Schmidt)	WIM
Rachmaninof	Sergei	Prelude Op. 3 Nr. 2 in C# Minor	Harlequin
Rachmaninof	Sergei	Vocalise (arr. A. Bailey)	Harlequin
Ravel	Maurice	Pièce en forme de Habanera (arr. Finno)	Kendor
Reed	Alfred	Clarinette Valsante (arr. D. McCathren)	Kendor
Reinhardt	D.	En Verdine (arr. Y. Bouchet)	IMD
R.-Korsakoff	Nikolaj	Hummelflug (arr. L. Caillet)	Southern
R.-Korsakoff	Nikolaj	Dance of the Buffoons (arr. G. F. Roach)	Southern
Roberts	Timothy	Toreador Song (arr. E. Vincent)	Southern
Roden	Robert R.	Difference of Opinion (1966)	Southern
Roden	Robert R.	Two Water Colors	Southern
Roden	Robert R.	Waltz and Beguine (1971)	Southern
Roost	Jan van der	Puszta (arr. M. Jense)	de haske
Roost	Jan van der	Rikudim. Vier israelische Volkstänze (arr. M. Jense) (1990)	de haske
Roovers	N.	Suite for Clarinet Choir	
Rossini	Gioacchino	Italian in Algiers (arr. H. G. Palmer)	Kendor
Rossini	Gioacchino	La Cenerentola Overture (arr. Anderson)	Jeanne
Rossini	Gioacchino	William Tell – Overture (arr. P. Harvey)	Harlequin
Runchak	Volodymyr	The Duel (1995)	Runchak
Sacci	Frank	Christmas Carol for Clar. Choir, 1 & 2	Kendor
Saint-Saens	Camille	Indroduction et Rondo Capriccioso (arr. A. Suppan)	Kliment
Saint-Saens	Camille	Romanze in F	Southern
Salter	Timothy	Heptad (1982)	Usk Edition
Salzedo		Canzona Op. 106 (1986)	Lopes
Sammlung		Christmas Carols (arr. F. Sacci) 2 Hefte	Kendor
Sammlung		Christmas Jazz Medley	Kendor
Sammlung		Clarinet Choir Repertoire by Voxman	Rubank
Sammlung		Robbins Collection of Classics for Balanced Clarinet Choir by Barnes	Big Three
Scarlatti	Domenico	The cat's fuge (arr. F. Thurston)	Southern
Scheidt	Samuel	Canzon super Intradam Aechiopicam (arr. C. Anderson)	Schirmer

Schickele	Peter	Monochrome III (1976)	E.-Vogel
Schmidt	William	The Turkish Lady	WIM
Schmidt	William	Vendor's Call (1976)	WIM
Schmitt	Florent	Sextuor op. 128	Billaudot
Shostakovich	Dimitri	2 Preludes (arr. W. Schmidt)	WIM
Schubert	Franz	Menuett und Trio (arr. Cl. W. Johnson)	Rubank
Schubert	Franz	Militärmarsch D-Dur, op. 51 (arr. A. Suppan)	Kliment
Schubert	Franz	Symphonie Nr. 5. Daraus: 1. Satz (arr. M. Walton)	Australian
Schumann	Robert	Etude, Op. 56, Nr. 5 (arr. R. Brown)	WIM
Schumann	Robert	Etude, Op. 56, Nr. 6 (arr. R. Brown)	WIM
Schumann	Robert	Fuge, Op. 60, Nr. 1 (arr. R. Brown)	WIM
Schumann	Robert	Paradise and the Peri (arr. Th. T. Donley)	Medici
Schumann	Robert	Serenade (arr. Bale)	Bale
Schumann	Robert	Sketch, Op. 58, Nr. 4 (arr. R. Brown)	WIM
Schwartz	Paul	Vienna Baroque Suite (arr. D. Hite) (1970)	Ludwig
Schwarz	Ira-Paul	Capriccio	Rubank
Scott	Ronald	Bagatelle Nr. 1	Cimarron
Searle	Humphrey	Divertimento op. 54 (1970)	Faber
Snavely	Jack	Motif and Variation (1967)	Kendor
Soenen	Willy	Dia y Noche	
Soenen	Willy	Variations on a Theme by one of Guido's Friends	
Sousa	John Philipp	Stars and Stripes forever (arr. L. Conley)	Kendor
Spaniola	Josef	Rocky Mountain Rising	
Spaniola	Josef	Sweet Light's Reflection	
Stamitz	Carl	Allegretto (arr. E. Del Borgo)	Kendor
Stamitz	Karl	Konzert Nr. 1 in F-Dur (arr. G. Dangain)	Billaudot
Steinberg	Paul	Ebonata (1980)	Kendor
Stevenson	Jennifer	Tempisne Edax Rerum	
Strauß	Johann	Perpetuum Mobile, Op. 257	Kendor
Strauß	Joh. & Josef	Pizzicato Polka (arr. J. Lancelot)	Billaudot
Strauß	Joh. & Josef	Pizzicato Polka (arr. J. Van der Goot)	Muzika

Strauß	Johann (Sohn)	Neue Steirische Tänze, op. 61 (arr. A. Suppan)	Kliment
Strauß	Johann	Radetzky-Marsch (arr. J. Lancelot)	Billaudot
Strauß	Johann	Radetzky-Marsch (arr. K. Schmid)	Kliment
Stravinsky	Igor	Ronde des Princesses (arr. W. Schmidt)	WIM
Sundell	Spencer	December Fog	Dorn
Susato	T.	Three Susato Dances (arr. D. Marlatt)	Eight Note
Tartini	Giuseppe	Concertino (arr. G. Jacob) (1969)	Boosey
Telemann	Georg Ph.	Largo und Presto aus der Suite (arr. Cl. Johnson)	Rubank
Telemann	Georg Ph.	Polonaise und Passepied (arr. Cl. W.Johnson)	Rubank
Thommessen	Olav Anton	Stanzas for Clarinet (1975)	Norsk
Tiensuu	Jukka	Vento	FIMIC
Traditional		Sinterklaas Potpourri (arr. J. v. der Goot)	Muzika
Traditional		When the Saints (arr. J. Christensen)	Kendor
Traditional		Dona nobis pacem (arr. E. Del Borgo)	Kendor
Traditional		Gay 90´s Jazz Suite (arr. L. Niehaus)	Kendor
Traditional		Irish Suite (arr. E. Del Borgo)	Kendor
Traditional		Londonderry air (arr. D. Casteel)	Kendor
Traditional		Spiritual Jazz Suite (arr. L. Niehaus)	Kendor
Traditional		Stephen Foster Jazz Suite (arr. L. Niehaus)	Kendor
Traditional		Yuletide Jazz Suite Nr. 1 (arr. L. Niehaus)	Kendor
Traditional		Yuletide Jazz Suite Nr. 2 (arr. L. Niehaus)	Kendor
Tschaikowsky	Peter I.	Andante Cantabile (arr. Cl. W. Johnson)	Rubank
Tschaikowsky	Peter I.	Canzonetta and Finale aus dem Violin-Konzert (arr. L. Cailliet) (1962)	Leblanc
Tschaikowsky	Peter I.	Dance of the Reed Pipes (arr. L. Conley)	Kendor
Tschaikowsky	Peter I.	Elegie (arr. N. H. Seward)	Wingert
Tschaikowsky	Peter I.	Finale (arr. L. Caillet)	Southern
Tschaikowsky	Peter I.	Marsch aus „Der Nußknacker" (arr. D. Kirkwood)	Iatona
Tschaikowsky	Peter I.	Mini Overture (arr. L. Conley)	Kendor

Tschaikowsky	Peter I.	Quartett. Daraus: Andante cantabile (arr. Cl. W. Johnson)	Rubank
Tschaikowsky	Peter I.	Romanze (arr. G. Lewin)	Harlequin
Tschaikowsky	Peter I.	Russischer Tanz aus "Der Nußknacker" (arr. R. Holder)	de haske
Tschaikowsky	Peter I.	Schwanensee. Daraus: Russischer Tanz (arr. R. Holder)	de haske
Tschaikowsky	Peter I.	Trepak (arr.L. Conley)	Kendor
Tschaikowsky	Peter I.	Waltz from Serenade for Strings (arr. F. Sacci)	Kendor
Uber	David	Andante and Danza	Southern
Uber	David	Interdiffussions and Scherzando	Kendor
Uber	David	Masques	Kendor
Uber	David	Musicale	Kendor
Uber	David	Parade	Southern
Uber	David	Three Settings for Clarinet Choir	Kendor
Vänskä	Osmo	Image	FIMIC
Verdi	Guiseppe	La Forza del Destino (arr. P. Harvey)	Harlequin
Villa-Lobos	Heitor	Aria aus Bachianas Brasileiras Nr. 5 (arr. J. Krance) (1971)	Associated
Vinter	Gilbert	Sextett	MS
Vivaldi	Antonio	Konzert für 2 Klarinetten. Daraus: 1. Satz (arr. M. Walton)	Australian
Vivaldi	Antonio	Konzert in Es-Dur, Nr. 28 (arr. K. Peters)	Belwin
Vivaldi	Antonio	Konzert in F-Dur, Nr. 36 (arr. K. Peters)	Belwin
Walters	Harold L.	Blue Twilight	Rubank
Walters	Harold L.	Valse a la scherzo	Rubank
Watts	Isaac	My Shepherd Will Supply My Need (arr. A. Rice-Young)	Alry Pub.
Webber	Andrew L.	The Phantom of the Opera (arr. J. van der Goot)	Muzika
Weber	Alain	Sextuor	MS
Weber	Carl Maria v.	Fantasia and Rondo (arr. N. Heim)	Shawnee
Weber	Carl Maria v.	Grand Duo Concertante (arr. M. Walton)	Australian

Weber	Carl Maria v.	Walz and Trio (arr. Wyver)	Hilltop
Werner	Jean-Jacques	Trois Paraphrases (1986)	Choudens
White	Gary	Convolutions (1982)	Kendor
Wilder	Alec	Suite for Clarinet Choir (1979)	Margun
Williams	Ralph V.	Rhosymedre (arr. P. Williams)	Jensen
Wilson	Brian	I get around (arr. C. Calvin)	Belwin
Woolfenden	Guy	Three Dances (1985)	Ariel
Yoder	Paul	Bach-Suite	Southern
Young	Donald	Kroyer Variations	Kendor
Young	Donald	Northern Legend	Kendor
Zabka	Stan & Upton	Christmas eve in my hometown (arr. C. Custer)	Belwin
Zamecnik	Evzen	Eine kleine Abendmusik	Rundig
Zingarelli	Nicola A.	Motet (arr. J. Verne)	Kendor

6.2   Works with Clarinet Choir Accompaniment

1. Title in alphabetical order, 2. Solo Instrument, 3. Grade of Difficulty,
4. Composer/Arranger

Title	Instrument	Grade	Composer/Arr.[157]
Allegro, KV 407	Horn	4	Mozart/Fischer
Allegro Maestoso	Horn	5	Mozart/Sacci
Andante and Scherzo	Clarinet	6	Gennaro
Andante and Rondo	Horn	5	Mozart/Sacci
Canzonetta	Alt Sax	4	Tschaikowsky/Cailliet
Concert Piece Nr. 1	2 Clarinets	5	Mendelssohn/Schwarz
Concerto in B-flat	Clarinet	5	Händel/Anderson
Concertino	Flute	5	Chaminade/Palmer-Heim
Concertino	Clarinet	5	Tartini/Jacob
Concerto in C, Op. 46, Nr. 1	2 Trumpets	6	Vivaldi/Yates
Concerto Saint Marc	Trumpet	5	Albinoni/Schmidt
Concerto	Clarinet	5	Graupner/Anderson
Concerto in F minor	C-Instrument	4	Händel/Anderson
Concerto Nr. 3	E flat Clarinet	5	Molter/Anderson
Fantasia and Rondo	Clarinet	4	Weber/Heim
Fantasies	3 Trumpets	4	Owen H.
Finale	Clarinet	5	Tschaikowsky/Cailliet
Flight of the Bumble Bee	Alt-Sax	5	Rimsky Korsakov/Cailliet

---

[157] cf. N. Heim (Ed.), 'Clarinet Choir. News International', Vol 7, Hyattsville, Maryland, 1982, pp. 8-9.

Intro & Concertante op.58	Bass Clarinet	4	Heim, N.
Lullaby	E flat Clarinet	5	Klauss, N.
Nuages	Alt-Sax	5	Debussy/Conley
Piece en Sol Mineur	3 Clarinets	4	Barat/Roach
Poem	Horn	6	Heim, N.
Prelude, Interlude & Scherzo	E flat Clarinet	5	Heim, N.
Red Rosy Bush	Alt-Sax	4	Cable, H.
Romance in F	Horn	4	Saint Saens/Cailliet
Rondo from Concerto	Trumpet	5	Hummel/Schmidt
The Brook	Bassoon	2	Organn
The Turkish Lady	Trumpet	5	Schmidt, W.
Untitled Poem	Flute/Piano	6	Rarig, H.
Vendor's Call	Piano	6	Schmidt, W.

6.3 Discography

As discographies tend not to be current for very long, I would rather point the reader in the direction of the numerous online CD shops, streaming services, social networks and online publishers and simply give a few recommendations.

If you are looking for Clarinet Choir recordings, I can wholeheartedly recommend the world's largest music streaming service/web portal for Classical Music, *Naxos Music Library*.[158]

You can also find fine performances and recommendations on the websites of *Harvey Hermann* (Illinois)[159] and *Mitchell Estrin* (Florida).[160]

In addition, the international clarinet trade magazine *The Clarinet* publishes a regular column entitled *Clarinet Cache*[161] (first issue June 2008) edited by Kellie Lignitz-Hahn and guest contributor Bret Pimentel which often includes links to excellent clarinet choirs and many interesting Repertoire Lists and recordings.[162]

---

[158] www.naxosmusiclibrary.com/ [accessed 27.07.2017]

[159] http://www.dfapam.com/clarinetchoir/ [accessed 27.07.2017]; cf. also Ch. 6.

[160] http://arts.ufl.edu/sites/clarinet-studio/uf-clarinet-ensemble/recordings/ [accessed 27.07.2017]

[161] cf. Kellie Lignitz Hahn, 'Clarinet Cache', in: *The Clarinet*, Vol. 35, No. 3, June 2008 et seq.

[162] cf. online edition www.clarinetcache.com/2016/03/clarinet-choirs.html

FSC
www.fsc.org
MIX
Papier | Fördert
gute Waldnutzung
FSC® C083411

Zeitfracht Medien GmbH
Ferdinand-Jühlke-Straße 7
99095 Erfurt, Deutschland
produktsicherheit@kolibri360.de